I Smiled BacK

THE STORY NOBODY KNOWS

Siobhán Mungovan

Book Hub Publishing

Printed in the European Union.

For more information, or to book an event, contact:
(Susan McKenna, Director and Commissioning Editor)
http://www.bookhubpublishing.com

Book design by Niall MacGiolla Bhuí
(ShadowScriptGhostwriters.Com)
Cover design by Niall MacGiolla Bhuí
(ShadowScriptGhostwriters.Com)

ISBN – Paperback : 978-1-7392899-4-2

First Edition : 2023

CONTENTS

Dedication

This book is dedicated to all the healthcare professionals that kept us safe during Covid-19. We are fortunate today in Ireland to have so many dedicated staff. I understand first-hand the incredible work they do each and every day and want to offer my heartfelt thank you to our frontline healthcare professionals in acute and critical care. Thank you for saving us, thank you for holding the hands of our loved ones who died without us by their sides, thank you for continuing to be there when we needed you, and thank you for caring!

Joseph Kelly
IG Account
josephkelly_art

FOREWORD

I'm a great believer in meeting people for a reason. 'I cannot think of an instance where this phrase has been truer, than when I met (or rather e-met), Siobhan in early 2021. She is a genuine jewel to anyone who has had the privilege to receive her time and energy. I've been honoured to get to know Siobhán over the past two years; the good, the hidden, the beauty, the brawn and the absolutely hilarious wit she holds.

When we first met, I was blown away by her knowledge, her compassion and her relentless inability to give up. It would put many a person to shame or, like me, it can prove as an inspiration. As a mental and emotional wellbeing coach, I did doubt myself and pondered over what I could possibly offer someone who was already so aware. As I had been working in social care and people-facing roles for over 17 years, I knew there would be a shadow area, a part of herself Siobhán hadn't yet tended to. I believe this book will show you the side of Siobhán that had not yet been uncovered, her gentleness with herself, her strength in her femininity and the love she found for what faces us all in the mirror, who she was inside and out. How many can say they have found this level of self-compassion?

But like most of us, Siobhán has had her own share of struggles and challenges to conquer and manage. In my opinion, this is where Siobhán really comes into her own. Her unwillingness to accept things as they are or as they are told by others is something to behold.

She soaks up information, gathers perspectives and analyses the situation constructively. You better believe that the next time she sits at the table with you, she'll have done her homework and she is about to show you what life can be, who she is and what she is not settling for.

Isn't this what we all want? Striving for better? Overcoming the challenges with learning and an 'I'll show you' attitude? Showing the world who we are without shame? And best yet, having a blooming good laugh as we go?

I hope that one day, I'll be as tenacious, gutsy and determined as this woman is now. Not only does Siobhán ooze gratitude for all that she is, has and holds, she strives for better every single day (even when she is told to rest but that's for another day). I believe her capacity and hunger for growth is also what lends her excess strength and courage to those who are facing similar challenges, physically, emotionally and mentally. Truly, she is the living, breathing version of 'borrow mine until you find your own'.

As you may already know or certainly will come to know, Siobhán has a different ability to the majority. In my opinion, this only enhances who she is. This adds to her experiences. This has given her different and probably, many more, challenges than the majority of us. Moreso,

Siobhán is not shy in coming forward about her challenges, on a personal level or on a far-reaching level through her writing in this book.

I cannot claim to know all the challenges Siobhán has encountered nor the full impact they have had on her, however, I draw from Siobhán something much more impactful by knowing parts of her story. I draw that the notion that adversity does not define you. I see that your support system whether this is family, friends or professionals, are a part of your backbone. I witness that you truly can have the experiences you desire, if only you believe in yourself enough to go after them. And finally, self-appreciation is something very worthy of our time and effort.

I believe that you will witness Siobhán's growth, expertise, experiences and self-compassion throughout this book and I hope that you will borrow some of hers until you find your own.

I'm privileged to be a part of her journey. We share laughs, tears and triumphs and bask in the glory of all of them.

Here's to us all achieving self-appreciation. Here's to our leader and guide, Siobhán.

—Shanna McSorley

About This Book

THE STORY NOBODY KNOWS

This photo represents the opening chapter. With this chapter, with this whole book, I want it to take you on a journey through the good times and the bad times. And with this photo, it represents somebody who has, and is still living a fulfilled life, even though they have had numerous challenges and obstacles put in their way.

This photo represents a woman, who has zest for life, a woman who has taken life and grabbed it by both hands and made the best of the situation and the life that she's been given.

It also represents personality and fun, with all life's challenges, but represented by love, by encouragement, by strength.

This photo shows the fun side to life. Life is difficult, there is no doubt about it. But also life is amazing. There's so much joy in life. This photo represents living in the present moment.

As humans, we spend so much time worrying about our past and being anxious about our future. But all we have is this present moment. It represents being present and soaking that up and being happy with what we have been given. It gives a sense of gratitude, you can see this from the smile; being happy with what you have been given. All too often in this life, we want more. We want bigger and better.

Being happy with the simple things in life is just as important and is the key message from me. The simple things in life are free but are also the most magical of gifts to be given.

A Publisher's Insight

THE STORY NOBODY KNOWS

A disability is a condition that limits a person's physical or mental abilities. Having a disability is similar to living in a castle with a moat around it; you are trapped within the castle unable to access the resources beyond the moat. No matter how strong the walls are, it doesn't provide the same freedom as crossing the bridge and being able to access the other side.

Prior to running an Indie Publishing House, I worked for over two decades in frontline supervision and management in social care across several disciplines. I've met many people who inspired me. The story of an Irish woman who lives with multiple disabilities is one of resilience, determination, and unwavering spirit in the face of adversity and is certainly inspiring. Despite the numerous challenges that this woman faces in her life, she persevered and inspired those around her with her courage and indomitable will. This is why I feel it is so important to publish this story about her life. In today's society, individuals with disabilities are often marginalised and excluded from mainstream society. It's terrible to say, but they are all-too-often perceived as a burden or as being unable to meaningfully contribute to society. However, the story of this Irish woman proves otherwise. Siobhán is a woman who is not just defined by her disabilities, but by her strengths, her passions, and her achievements. Through her life story, we can all gain insight into the resilience and courage that people with disabilities possess, and we can learn how they can overcome the many obstacles they face. Siobhán's life story is also a testament to the impact of supportive and inclusive communities.

Despite the many barriers she faces, she remains able to thrive, I believe, because of the love and support of her family, friends, and community. This demonstrates the crucial importance of creating and maintaining a society that is inclusive and supportive of individuals with disabilities, and it serves as a call to action for all of us to work towards building a more inclusive world. Moreover, by publishing her story we can help to dispel the myths and stereotypes that surround individuals with disabilities. Siobhán's life story shows that people with disabilities can lead extraordinary lives.

In addition to its educational and inspirational value, this biography is also a celebration of the human spirit. Siobhán's life story is a testament to the strength of the human will and the power of determination. By sharing her story, we can pay tribute to her legacy and to the legacy of all individuals with disabilities who have overcome adversity.

The publication of Siobhán's story is of immense importance because it highlights the courage and achievements of an Irish woman with multiple disabilities. It serves as a call to action for all of us to work towards creating a more inclusive and supportive world for individuals with disabilities, and it serves as a tribute to the human spirit and the power of determination. By sharing her story, we can help to dispel myths and stereotypes, and to inspire future generations to lead lives that are filled with hope, joy, and purpose.

Photography serves as an important form of visual documentation, allowing us to capture and remember special moments that would otherwise be forgotten. It allows us to share our experiences with others, and to look back fondly on special memories. Photos can bring back powerful emotions and memories that we might have forgotten.

Photos also provide a compelling and powerful way to communicate, allowing us to share our experiences with others, and to tell stories that would otherwise remain untold. By using photography, we can create a lasting legacy that can be appreciated for generations to come. It offers a unique perspective on our lives, that can never be replicated in any other way. According to Photutorial data, 1.2 trillion photos were taken worldwide in 2021, and this number is projected to increase to 2 trillion by 2025. In this book, we've added a few more. But, gosh, are these powerful.

—Susan McKenna,
  Director, The Book Hub Publishing Group, Galway and
    Limerick, Ireland.

*Gratitude to photographer Yvonne McTiernan for her fabulous captures of Siobhán for this book.

CHAPTER 1

THE STORY NOBODY KNOWS: THE PHOTOSHOOT

This picture represents why I did the photoshoot. You can clearly see in my eyes and my facial expression, that I'm thinking inwardly and throughout this shoot, that is exactly what I was doing, thinking inwardly. Working through my thoughts and emotions. Throughout the shoot, I expressed numerous different emotions. You can see photos where I'm smiling. You can see photos where I'm protecting myself. You can also see photos where I'm showing my vulnerability. And that is exactly what this photo represents. Showing my vulnerability for probably the first time to some people in society. I'm seen as a tough nut, the person who can get through anything. But in this photo, it says the opposite. It shows sheer vulnerability.

I really wanted to show that it's okay to be vulnerable because I do think sometimes, when there are elements wrong with our bodies, that we have to build up this tough exterior. It took me years to build up that exterior and years to break it down. We feel that we have to pretend that we're okay and that everything's alright. Sometimes the brutal truth is that things are not okay, and things are not alright. But that doesn't mean that you're not going to get through it, because you are going to get through it. I knew I just had allow myself to feel all of those emotions and that is exactly what I had to feel going through the photo shoot and I got a whole heap of it. This picture shows that I'm looking inwardly, I am not focusing outwardly. I'm focusing my attention and processing my emotions inwardly and throughout the photo shoot this is what I did. This photo represents 'my why'. 'My why' is focusing inwardly and not focusing so much on my outer shell. Holding my chest, protecting my heart, protecting my soul.

I feel it's really important to publish my story as a woman with disabilities who has done the unthinkable; I've completed and survived a naked photoshoot! Now, a naked photo shoot can be either really embarrassing or really empowering, especially if you have what might be considered obvious physical disabilities and not the 'normal' body that we have become used to showcasing in all the glamour magazines. It can be a way to reclaim the body and to show that beauty is not necessarily the same for everyone. Of course it isn't!

During that shoot I brought a full suitcase of clothes with me, I was so anxious about what I might feel and my clothes felt like a bit of a protection blanket. Imagine bringing a suitcase of clothes to a naked photoshoot! They were my security pieces, I needed them to help me push through the fear of it all. I wasn't sure I would even go through with it to be honest, I felt exposed and vulnerable, but I wanted to find the strength to show who I really am. We started off really gently and I was able to go at my own pace.

I cried sometimes during the shoot simply because I knew how important it was for me to do it and I had so much internal resistance to get past in order to do it. I did a lot of the shoot in silence. I didn't just jump in and strip off, I took my time. The whole shoot took 6 hours. That's quite a long time to be feeling the way I was! It was both exhausting and rewarding in ways I hadn't expected. I slept for 12 straight hours after that shoot, I was drained but also invigorated. It was a huge turning point for me, not a cure-all, but a moment in time that allowed me to show myself in the most raw way I ever had. I'm incredibly grateful to Yvonne, the photographer, for understanding that I needed her to be patient with me. She gave me the time and space to work through what I needed to in order to be able to actually do it. She didn't push me, but she held my hand and walked me through it. I felt that she was by my side the entire time, not pushing me or minimising how difficult it really was for me to see it through. I had to dig deep to find the courage and without her, I doubt it would have happened. That's the power of having people around me who understand and are willing to see things through with me, even though it may not always be easy for me to do things. I have a lot inside me that I have to share and show the world and having people around me who will take the time to work with me is such a gift.

In a way, it was a wakeup call for me. I don't see my back, I can't see it the same way that other people do because it's behind me. So when I saw some of pictures as we went along, I was in shock.

The severity of my disfigurement was really apparent. I was never treated differently growing up, apart from once being called a humpback which was really hurtful for me. I wouldn't wish that feeling on anybody. So to see myself quite literally stripped back to basics was a bit of a shock. On the other hand, I wanted to see the beauty in myself and of my body. It's hard to admit to ourselves that we are beautiful and even harder for me, but I did feel it. I could see how these pictures are a work of art. They brought up every insecurity I've ever had from my past and I slowly and quietly worked through each one all while the camera was clicking. It took everything I had within me to sit there and allow myself to be photographed. I couldn't imagine them being out there for the world to see but I want them to be seen. I want people to see that disability is beautiful too, it just looks different to what people are used to. It was one of the most challenging and rewarding things I have ever done.

I was once asked to do a fashion show and it was one of most exciting thoughts of my life to get my hair and make-up done professionally. A fashion show wasn't something I ever thought I would be asked to do. I was used to hiding my body to a certain degree, so being on a runway wasn't something I had ever contemplated. I was on cloud nine imagining what I might look like and how the day would go. It seemed so glamorous and enticing. I had always had fashion magazines growing up and loved looking at the styles.

I take pride in the fact that my clothes and my dress sense has always been quite modern and fashionable. I enjoy doing my makeup and my face has always been well presented. One thing I will say is that my hair has always been a security blanket for me. We all have our little comforts that we use when we feel a bit anxious, things we feel we can use to shield us from any comments about our body. For me, it's my hair. When I have it down, it covers my back and although it might sound silly, it makes me feel that others can't see my disability. It just protects me in that moment when I feel I need it, which isn't all the time. It's always been a blanket that I use to cover me when I don't want to feel exposed. So, you can imagine my horror when I get into the fashion show shoot and hear that the brief is 'red lips and hair tied up'. I froze in shock. How can I allow my hair to be up? That would mean everyone will be able to see my back and will be taking photographs of me.

All throughout the time that my hair is being pinned up, all I can think of is how am I going to do this with people I don't know. I was shaking like a leaf as my moment to make an appearance came closer. I questioned my sanity around agreeing to do this in the first place, was I crazy for putting myself out there like this? Is there time to back out now? Could I bring myself to do this in front of everyone?

As I made my way to the runway, I could hear laughing and joking and the clicking of cameras. I felt like my whole world was coming crashing down around me and I realised I had a choice to run, or to stay and do this. I knew I would have to let go of my security blanket and I wasn't sure I was ready or able. Perhaps if I had more time to prepare, but I was taken by surprise. My stomach was churning, my heart was pounding and I was sweating. I had very little time to make a choice, but whatever choice I made would shape how I felt about myself and my ability to push through fears. As I've said before, I've never been one for backing down in the face of a challenge, I'm stubborn, so I pulled on that strength this time too.

Whatever power I found within myself that day, helped me to do it. I realised that they were chanting my name and as I made my way down the runway, all I could feel is that I can't enjoy the moment because I'm so terrified of what they all must be thinking. I'm wondering if they are looking at my face or my back and I'm so consumed by what everyone else is thinking of me. As I get to the end, I turn and strike a pose as best as I can. I am flooded with relief in that moment, not that it's coming to an end but relief that I managed to do it. Relief mixed with a sense of pride in myself. I had managed to do something I had no control over and to find the strength within me to show the world who I am. That was a very important milestone for me, I faced a huge fear and came out the other side.

Now I'm not saying that I've never felt anxious about my body since then, because I have. It wasn't a fix-all situation, but it did improve my confidence a lot. I'm proud of myself for what I achieved that day. The feedback I got was incredible, people were genuinely happy for me that I had got up there and had showed the world who I really am. I really hoped that it shifted some perceptions around what is beautiful. Beauty comes in all forms and just because I have these disabilities and am not what might be considered conventionally beautiful, I wanted to show what is unique about me. I wanted to ask the people there to look at beauty in a different way than they were used to. I think I achieved that.

So I guess the moral of the story for me is that although we might all have something we use as a security blanket to wrap around ourselves, we can find the resources within to let it fall to the ground and let ourselves be seen by world. Allowing ourselves to be photographed in all our rawness isn't easy but it can be a way to help ourselves to heal all the insecurities we have, to work through the fears we have of being seen for who we are. It's just one of the ways to do this, there are many, but for me it was the most powerful and transformative.

It can also be a way to show that having a disability or, indeed, several disabilities does not have to mean being ashamed of one's body. It can be a way to feel empowered and to show that despite the disability, one is still beautiful. By showing that beauty comes in all shapes and forms, it can help to break down social norms and to make people more comfortable with themselves. It can help to build self-confidence and to make people feel more comfortable in their own skin. For example, when Gigi Hadid, a well-known model, appeared in the British Vogue wearing a prosthetic arm, it generated a lot of positive attention, and showed that beauty comes in all shapes and sizes.

Why did I do this you might ask? Don't worry, I've asked myself that many times and when I first mentioned it to my editor, Susan, I was filled with trepidation. But, she smiled and immediately replied, 'Well done you! And, sure, why would you not have done so?'. I took courage from this and so you'll find some of my 'photoshoot day photos' throughout this book. But, more of this again.

To be honest, I did the photoshoot because I wanted to challenge the stereotypes about what beauty is and highlight the importance of valuing *all* bodies, regardless of (supposed) ability. In addition to promoting body positivity and self-empowerment, a naked photo shoot also helps to raise awareness about the *experiences* of individuals with disabilities.

Many people may not fully understand the challenges faced by someone like me with my disabilities, such as the physical limitations I face daily – including getting ready for each individual photo as I was required to move and contort myself into different positions. I hope to have given a face and a voice to these experiences and help to educate others about the importance of genuine inclusivity and understanding.

It took a lot of courage for me to pose for the photos, but I knew they would be an essential part of my message with this book. It's one thing reading about a woman with a disability and quite another to be able to see that same woman visually, with very little clothes on. I want them to be impactful, raw and honest. They represent a disabled woman in society with a disfigurement, and I want be seen in my true beauty for what I am and to be taken seriously in society for my sexuality.

Representation in society is lacking when it comes to people with severe disfigurements. And that is why I want people to see the photos, even though they're beautiful photos, some of them are uncomfortable to look at.

I want people to get comfortable with the uncomfortable. I want people to know that it's okay to be to be nervous, it's okay to have these fears and not know about disfigurement.

I want to get the message across that it's not to be brushed under the carpet and to be ignored. So that's why the photos are very, very important. The visual attribute is just as important as the written story.

I was determined that the pictures would break the patterns of people with disabilities being seen as a shell and that shell doesn't fully represent the true self that I am.

Often, people automatically judge the outward shell they see, because I suppose when you have your clothes on, you have your 'dress up' on. Nobody can really see the truth and the severity of it. It's not that people mean to be judgemental, but they often don't understand what they can't see. I wanted to change that, even if it is shocking at first.

An important thing I wanted to get across with this book, is that it's okay to show vulnerability, because for me to actually build up the courage to do the photoshoots really took me to that really vulnerable state. After everything I've been through, it wasn't easy to put myself out there like that and risk ridicule or rejection. I doubted my own bright ideas about it at times, but in the end I thought the message that I was trying to portray was a lot more important than the possibility of it not going down well.

It has taken me quite some time to allow myself to do it. I decided to try and portray different parts of my personality in the photos, I wanted people to see that I have more to me than being the girl with a disability. My hope with showing these photos to people is that they begin to see that a disability doesn't have to define us, it isn't all we are.

I suppose particularly in this day and age, everything is photoshopped, everything is filtered. Everyone seems to strive for the perfect beautiful body and sometimes, anything other than that isn't acceptable. I wanted these pictures to break down the perceptions of what is beautiful and what is not. I wanted to show that just because a body looks different, that doesn't mean it doesn't have beauty in its own right.

There's a huge amount of perfectionism out there in society and here I come to the forefront, with all my bumps and nooks and crannies. I'm proud of my body, it's not the perfect body in any way shape or form, but it's got me to the age of 36 against all odds, so why not celebrate that? Let's all celebrate our bodies for getting us where we are today.

I'm showing the severity of my disability, but my personality comes shining through too. That's my body, my shell, but it's my soul and my smile you see in those pictures.

In some of my pictures, I want people to see that I didn't lie down and accept what was told to me at face value. I want you to see the warrior in me. In others, I want people to see the ways I'm protecting myself and taking care of myself. I guess you could say that's the more vulnerable side of me represented.

It's not that I want to influence anyone with my pictures, but my hope is that a young adult or a teen could look at those photos and know that they can be perceived as beautiful, even if it is in a completely different way. It took me so long to come to terms with accepting my body for what it is, if I can help someone along the road on their journey then I've done my job well.

I want society to be able to open up to those opportunities, and to be able to see that and for them to be proud of their body and not have to hide it away. I spent too many years hiding away and being ashamed of my body. I know I don't need to do that anymore. Getting these pictures done really helped me with that, I'm so glad I pushed myself to do it despite my fears. I feel like a much more confident woman now and it feels good to be in touch with my sexuality.

I don't allow myself to be uncomfortable in order to fit in with my peers. I had to look inwards, and it's probably one of the scariest things we can do. If you keep looking to the external world for approval, you will never reach that state of contentment with yourself. I've done a lot of work on that in the last 7 years.

I didn't do the photos to try and fit in with everyone else. I want them to show my uniqueness. I rejected my scoliosis for years. I remember one night making a wish on a shooting star, that my scoliosis would disappear. It's just amazing to me that I'm such a different person from that now and I'm in a much better place. When I was 15, I would have done anything for my scoliosis to disappear. But now I can see how hard my body has worked, and how far it's gotten me to being a 36-year-old. It's unheard of and it's okay to say that. I don't say that was with sadness. I've gotten to the age of 36. This is something to be celebrated.

So I am celebrating my body. Yes, it's completely different to yours. But everybody's different. Everybody's body is different. Nobody's body is the same. I fear that's what social media has done to us. Social media has said that one type of body is the only type of body that's going to be accepted in society. And that's it, if you don't fit into that bracket, you might as well just quietly do your laundry or go away and start crying. That is slowly changing, thank goodness, as more people with disabilities step up and do things like this. By doing what I'm doing, I'm hoping that I'm showing that there are other types of bodies; curved, skinny, and so much more. We haven't seen disfigurement, and that's why I'm truly passionate about putting it to the forefront.

I'm one of the first to do this, there is another girl in England that I saw a few years ago, doing the same thing, pushing her scoliosis to the forefront. She is making it part and parcel of who she is instead of rejecting it. I think I relate to her in a lot of aspects.

Going through the same things, perhaps both of us losing our mobility and going through that grieving process. It showed me that there are people out there in the same boat as me. 'When it comes to my strength, I get it from my mom. She had to develop her own strength very quickly when she had a child with Spina Bifida with Hydrocephalus.

I had to tell my mom about the pictures, just in case someone from down the road did. We live in the country so someone might have mentioned them to her if I didn't. I didn't want her to be surprised. I told her everything was done with taste, but that there might be bits that she might be uncomfortable with. I think by now she understands that I'm trying to help others as well as myself. I'm trying to get a message out there. A message about loving our body regardless of what it looks like.

It also sends a powerful message to us all about self-love and confidence, showing that anyone with disabilities can celebrate their bodies and feel beautiful. Beauty is not defined by the physical appearance of any one individual but is instead created by how we *feel* and how we choose to express ourselves.

It encourages us to accept and appreciate all bodies, regardless of their physical capabilities.

To cite an interesting example, the Paralympic Games has become a platform for disabled athletes to showcase their abilities and to challenge the traditional definitions of what it means to be physically capable.

Here's what I think; Ideas of what is 'beautiful' are very often socially constructed, especially by fashion magazines and advertising. What is considered 'beautiful' is based on what society has deemed acceptable. This is often determined by those in power who create the images and messages we see in magazines and advertisements which can lead to unrealistic expectations when it comes to beauty, as well as feelings of inadequacy for those who don't conform to these standards.

This can have a detrimental effect on people's self-esteem and mental health. Consequently, I think it's ok to argue that it is important to recognise the potential harm of these unrealistic beauty standards and to actively challenge them in order to protect the mental well-being of all individuals.

For instance, one way to challenge them is to support body-positive influencers and campaigns that encourage people to celebrate their individuality and recognise beauty in all shapes and sizes.

Body positivity is the idea that all people should have a positive body image, meaning they accept and appreciate their own bodies. This includes people of all shapes, sizes, and abilities. The Paralympic Games is similar to a megaphone for those with disabilities, amplifying their voices and giving them a platform to be seen, heard, and appreciated for their abilities and contributions to sport.

The #LoveYourLines campaign on Instagram celebrates stretch marks and aims to normalise them by showing the beauty of all body types. In addition, to promoting inclusivity, it is important to challenge unrealistic beauty standards by actively supporting messages that promote self-love and acceptance. By challenging these standards, this campaign is creating a supportive community that celebrates the natural beauty of everyone. Another example of an inclusive messaging campaign is the #MyBeautyMySay hashtag, which encourages people to speak up about the beauty standards and labels that society places on them.

Body positivity is a movement that seeks to challenge the prevailing societal norms and expectations around physical appearance, particularly in regard to size and shape and is beoming a more dominant force across all social media platforms. It encourages individuals to embrace their bodies, flaws and all, and reject negative self-talk and feelings of shame.

Although the movement has gained traction in recent years, it still faces opposition and resistance from those who believe in traditional beauty standards.

It must also be noted that the body positivity movement has often been criticised for being exclusive and not inclusive of individuals with disabilities. So, that fact that a 36-year-old woman participated in a naked photo shoot is helping to break down these barriers, while sending a powerful message about the importance of body positivity for all individuals, regardless of their abilities.

Inclusivity is the practice of providing equal opportunities for all people, regardless of race, ethnicity, age, gender, sexual orientation, or any other characteristic. Inclusivity is like a well-cooked meal that can nourish everyone, regardless of their dietary preferences or restrictions.

It is a warm, welcoming environment that respects and celebrates the individuality of every single person. According to McKinsey's Delivering Through Diversity report, corporations that embrace gender diversity on their executive teams are more competitive and 21% more likely to experience above-average profitability. They also had a 27% likelihood of outperforming their peers on longer-term value creation.

So, this is a book that charts the personal journey of a 36-year-old Irish woman who has a number of disabilities including scoliosis, kidney malfunction and reduced lung capacity. This woman is me. It follows my journey over the years as I navigate the world with my disabilities. I'll discuss how I cope with the day-to-day challenges I face, how I find strength and resilience in the face of adversity. My message in this book is, you can too. Keep smiling always, as you are beautiful from the inside out and your true power lies within you.

Through my journey, I have been able to discover how to take advantage of the best of my circumstances and I've also been able to develop tools to help me overcome my obstacles. I am empowered to recognise my own worth, value, and potential, and to truly realise that my disabilities do not define me. You and I are much more than this. Much, much more.

By learning to rely on my own inner strength, I am independent. I have, over time, developed a newfound appreciation for myself and my abilities and I have learned to embrace my uniqueness and potential. I have also found a sense of purpose in my unique gifts and talents, and I am more confident about pursuing them.

As I have grown in self-awareness, I have been able to identify areas where I need help and support, but I am able to advocate for myself in order to get it. This allows me to make more informed decisions and take control of my own life. My own values and beliefs help to guide my decisions in a way that aligns with what I truly want out of life. Additionally, I'm now much more aware of my own boundaries, and I can at least try to make sure that I am not taken advantage of or pushed into anything that I'm not comfortable with.

This is similar to you seeing a roadmap of your life for the first time. You can now navigate your own journey, avoiding any detours that might take you away from your destination, while having the ability to stop to take in the scenery along the way.

I have to stay true to my values and my core ethos when it comes to why I'm doing this book. I don't know where I got this idea of leaving a legacy behind me. I've always said that. I said that about my last book as well, I just want to leave something behind that touched somebody's life. It doesn't have to be anybody in particular, just someone who needs to read it or see the pictures to help them comes to terms with who they are and what they are experiencing. I want to show the importance of the people who touch my life. I want them to know I see all the hard work they've put in. I want to acknowledge all they've put up with from me. I just want to say 'Guys, it hasn't gone unnoticed'. I do think with this book, that it's been achieved quite beautifully.

CHAPTER 2

LIFE WITH DISABILITIES

This photo represents life with disabilities. Throughout this chapter, we will go into detail about what spina bifida is and all that comes with this condition, in the medical world.

It's okay to sit with those emotions. Those emotions are just as important as any other emotions. With that, I'd like to draw your attention to the eyes.

The eyes represent that there's light at the end of the tunnel. You can see by this photo that I'm looking forward, I'm not looking backwards. Because even though the last 36 years of my life have been somewhat of a roller coaster, there's been good days, there's been bad days, there have been struggles, but also celebrations. And throughout this book, I choose to celebrate life. Yes, it's been difficult. But I have had an amazing support network, an amazing family, who have gotten me through those bad times. They have helped me build my character. I'm extremely thankful for the fact they've helped me build resilience. They've helped me build coping mechanisms. They have helped me to know, deep down inside, that even though I go through hard times, I will get through them, no matter what. They have helped me with that core self-belief.

I'm speaking to each and every single person in this photo that has a disability, whether it's Spinal Bifida or not, you can and you will achieve anything in your life, once you put your all into it, you must put your heart and soul into what you want to achieve. I'm also speaking to the parents, who may have just been given the gift of having a child with special needs. It's going to be one hell of a journey of believing in yourself as a parent. You can, and you will be able to do this. Believe in your child. And the one thing I will say is never underestimate what your child is going to achieve 5/10 years down the road. Because your child is beautiful, from the inside out, no matter what anybody has to say.

I want to draw your attention to the sense of contentment in this photo. Even though it has taken me years to get to a sense of contentment. All the hard work that I have put into myself has been well worth it. That's the scary part. Sometimes we don't want to put the work into ourselves. Because we are afraid to see what will come to the surface. But I can honestly say from the bottom of my heart, it's been the most rewarding thing ever.

Yes, a life with disabilities is difficult. But it's also a gift. It's a gift in a sense that has given me sense of gratitude for the things I have in life. It has helped me to focus my attention on what I can do, rather than what I can't. It has focussed my attention to what I have in life. What I don't have. It has given me a sense of appreciating the little things in life. It has given me the drive to appreciate every single day.

This book is all about celebrating. Celebrating life and celebrating your journey of what you've been through. So, if you are to get one thing from this book, I want you to see the fire that is within. The fire that is within each and every single one of you. And as I always say, 'Never underestimate the human potential'.

A disability is a condition that limits a person's physical or mental abilities. The most common types of disabilities are:

1. Attention Deficit Hyperactivity Disorder (ADHD) 2. Learning Disabilities. 3. Mobility Disabilities. 4. Medical Disabilities. 5. Psychiatric Disabilities. 6. Traumatic Brain Injury (TBI) and Post-Traumatic Stress Disorder (PTSD) 7. Visual Impairments. 8. Deaf and Hard of Hearing.

What about me? Well, I have Spina Bifida with Hydrocephalus. I also have Kyphoscoliosis which is scoliosis from the front and back. I have kidney failure of which I have 10% kidney function. I also have 10% lung capacity due to my kyphoscoliosis. Lucky me, eh? This is why I say 10 is my lucky number. It really is.

Here's the science bit over the next few pages so, no pun intended, brace yourselves! Spina Bifida is a type of birth defect that affects the spinal cord and the bones surrounding it. It occurs when the spinal column doesn't close properly during prenatal development, resulting in damage to the spinal cord and nerves. Hydrocephalus, on the other hand, is a condition where there is an accumulation of fluid in the brain, causing an increase in pressure inside the skull.

Spina Bifida can range from mild to severe, and in some cases, it can be accompanied by hydrocephalus. This is because the fluid build-up in the brain can put pressure on the spinal cord, causing further damage.

So, you might ask, what causes Spina Bifida and Hydrocephalus? While the exact cause is unknown, a range of studies have shown that a combination of genetic and environmental factors can play a role. For example, it wasn't well known for a long time that women who don't get enough folic acid before and during pregnancy are at a higher risk of having a baby with Spina Bifida. Other factors that have now been shown to also increase the risk include family history, exposure to certain chemicals, and certain medical conditions.

In terms of symptoms, it can vary depending on the severity of the condition. For those with mild Spina Bifida, they may not experience any noticeable symptoms. However, for those with more severe cases, they may experience things like loss of sensation, muscle weakness, and problems with bladder and bowel control.

For people with Hydrocephalus, symptoms may include headache, vomiting, irritability, and in severe cases, intellectual disability and, of course, some people with Hydrocephalus may not have any symptoms at all.

So, what happens when someone is diagnosed with Spina Bifida and Hydrocephalus? Well, there's no cure for either condition, but there are treatments that can help manage the symptoms and improve quality of life. For example, surgery can be used to close the opening in the spinal column and prevent further damage to the spinal cord. In terms of Hydrocephalus, a shunt may be inserted to help drain the excess fluid from the brain and relieve pressure.

In addition to these medical treatments, there are also a number of therapies and assistive devices that can help individuals with Spina Bifida and Hydrocephalus. For example, physical therapy can help improve mobility and strengthen muscles, while assistive devices like braces and wheelchairs can make it easier for individuals to get around.

It's important to note that even with the best care and treatments, Spina Bifida and Hydrocephalus can have a significant impact on an individual's life. This can range from physical challenges, like difficulty with mobility and bladder control, to emotional and psychological challenges, like feelings of isolation and low self-esteem.

Kyphoscoliosis, which is a fancy way of saying a combination of a spinal curve disorder (kyphosis) and another curve disorder (scoliosis). This condition can result in a humpback appearance and sideways curvature of the spine, and it can be a real pain in the back... literally!

Kyphoscoliosis can affect people of all ages, but it is most commonly diagnosed in children and adolescents. It can be caused by a variety of things, including genetic conditions, congenital disorders, and even poor posture. It can also develop as a result of other underlying medical conditions such as osteoporosis or muscular dystrophy.

The symptoms of kyphoscoliosis can vary depending on the severity of the condition, but some common ones include back pain, limited mobility, difficulty breathing, and uneven shoulders or hips. In severe cases, the curvature of the spine can put pressure on the lungs and heart, which can lead to respiratory and cardiovascular issues.

So, what can be done about kyphoscoliosis? There are several treatment options available, depending on the severity of the condition. For mild cases, physical therapy and exercises to improve posture and strengthen the back muscles can be effective. In more severe cases, a back brace may be needed to help support the spine and prevent further curvature.

Surgery is another option for people with kyphoscoliosis, and it can be very effective in correcting the spinal curvature. The type of surgery will depend on the individual case, but some common procedures include spinal fusion, which involves fusing two or more vertebrae together, and vertebral column resection, which involves removing a portion of the vertebral column to alleviate pressure on the spinal cord. Surgery was never an option for me, for various reasons. I came to terms with the idea that I didn't need something fixed in order to love myself and that I was ok as I am. It took me years to come to that point of acceptance of my conditions without always looking for the next fix, but when I did, it was the one true thing that healed me on the inside. My whole ethos is that we don't need to fix things about ourselves in order to fit in, to be loved or to be an important part of the world. In any case, the waiting list for surgery is extremely long, especially for people of school age. That meant that even if I had been a candidate for surgery, I would have had a very long and possibly anxious wait anyway.

It's worth mentioning that kyphoscoliosis can also have a significant impact on a person's self-esteem and confidence. Being self-conscious about a noticeable spinal curve can be really difficult to deal with – especially in such a pervasive social media climate, which I will come back to later in this book.

It's important that I say how much respect I have for the medical community that have helped me over the years. I will mention this throughout my book, because without them, I wouldn't have the quality of life that I'm able to have now with the conditions that I've just talked about. I really have been very lucky with my experiences of the medical system. I know not everyone can say the same, but for me, I feel very blessed with the professionals who have helped me. It's hard to hear about other people with disabilities who haven't been as lucky as me. I hear about people who are spoken over, not taken seriously, by-passed and treated with a terrible lack of respect. Not to mention the damage that can be done when there is simply a lack of knowledge and understanding around the disability from the medical professionals' side, which can lead to poorer outcomes for the patient and a feeling of being short-changed.

Sometimes, there is simply a fear of people with disabilities within a medical setting, as this setting isn't used to dealing with these types of conditions on a daily basis. For example, I had to go into A&E once and that's one setting where the doctors may not be used to dealing with someone with my issues. I was there for hours, and that was fine, I didn't mind the wait and was as patient as I always am. When my turn arrived, I could see the doctor on call walking up to the nurse's station to collect the file for his next patient. The nurse talked to him for a while and I noticed she was pointing at me, telling him that I was next.

What struck me straight away, and what I had expected to see, was the sheer fear on his face when he saw me. It was a look that said, 'What am I supposed to do here'? I've seen that look on faces of lots of people over the years, not just in the medical profession. I don't mind it, as I understand that it may be daunting for people if they haven't met me before or don't know much about my conditions.

The nurse was trying to talk to him and let him know that I knew my stuff about my own medical history. She tried to let him know that I knew what was going on and was perfectly capable of talking to him about it.

So when he came to me, he approached me with such care and attention and told me we could go really slowly and at my own pace. Me being me, I just launched into my whole medical history, giving him all the information that he might need and more. The poor fella was probably overwhelmed by me, but it was obvious to him that I could hold my own. That's the thing with me, I can talk about it all with confidence and be myself. That comes with years of experience with being in hospitals and going to all sorts of medical appointments. I've always said the person with any medical condition is the most qualified person in the room. I personally feel sometimes doctors see a disability or a condition as if it's something you can read off a textbook, which of course has its place. I am a science kinda girl myself but if I was to say one thing to any up and coming doctors it's that the person with the disability is living and breathing this condition every day of the week. So, no matter what words you throw at them, when it comes to their condition, they will understand what it means to them. The lived experience is priceless and if the doctor takes the time to understand the patient in front of them and not the one in the text book they will be pleasantly surprised that they very often know a hell of a lot more than the doctor might have thought.

I spent years in and out of these types of situations and it taught me to find my own voice, I had to speak for myself, on my own behalf, as much as I could. To be able to do that is one thing that I can actually have control over when it comes to my body. There's absolutely nothing wrong with my cognitive ability, and that's one thing that people don't know about me until they listen to me talk. Sometimes I can see the shock and relief on their faces that I'm able to speak for myself in such a way.

Often the perception of people with physical disabilities is that there must be something wrong with our minds and abilities to communicate effectively. I struggle with that perception and assumption. I often come up against it and have made it my life's work to challenge it.

It happens to me on a regular basis that people will assume I have difficulty with communication and I want to teach people not to judge a book by its cover. That's my motto really. Don't judge me by how I look. I'm well able to deal with any discussions around my health or anything else. I like surprising people with that, it's one area of my life where I feel I have relative control.

Not everyone has the opportunity to be listened to and heard in general, including as a patient. I'm grateful for the doctors who spend time listening to me, the ones who really listen to my story and my opinions, wishes and desires around my own health. One doctor said to me in a very direct and honest way, that he had never had a patient like me before and that he had no idea where to start. I admired that transparency, and to this day, he's the one I have the most solid confidence in. He sat with me and simply said that although he didn't know how to begin, that we would get through it together. He validated what I had to say and took me seriously. That meant the world to me as so many people throughout my life have operated in a different way. I think that's why I can sometimes come across as really straight talking and to the point, I've had to be to make sure that I'm heard and that people look past my physical disabilities to hear my voice properly. I do think people are surprised when I'm able to speak up for myself and to stand up for right and wrong. I just want to help others find their voice in that way, to find the confidence to speak out about their needs and desires and opinions. Everyone deserves to be taken seriously in my opinion, no matter what physical issues they have going on. I never want anyone to have to deal with the feeling of not being able to speak up for their beliefs. When I was younger, I would have felt that I might get into trouble for speaking up but as I always say, I'm a work in progress, so I've become more outspoken with age.

Time is short, use it wisely and be yourself. That's what I tell myself on a daily basis if I come up against any internal resistance.

Once I was going into hospital for an appointment and I was met at the door by a male nurse who was going to check me in. I went into pure diva mode, I'm embarrassed to admit. I demanded to know where the doctor was who I was due to see, I told the nurse the doctor had promised to meet me at the door and demanded that he come. The poor nurse was quite shocked and a bit put out to say the least. I know myself well enough to say that when I'm feeling afraid and vulnerable, I can go into that diva mode a bit. It's a method of self-protection. I had hoped that doctor would meet me at the door because I was feeling a bit exposed and I didn't really want to be there. So I froze and sort of lashed out. I catch myself doing that when I don't feel 100% on form. Needless to say I had to come back with my tail between my legs and apologise. It wasn't my finest moment. Honestly, that's an element of dealing with disabilities that a lot of people don't understand, we can tend to feel vulnerable a bit more than others in certain situations. I hope that we are forgiven for that, it's not always easy and I have my off days too.

On the other hand, there are times when I'm given special treatment that other people wouldn't get. For example, when I was in school, I got away with things that I doubt anybody else did. I don't in any way condone taking time off school to go shopping, but one day I did. I should have been in class but decided to go into town instead. I didn't do it often, but on this particular day I just wanted to get out and about. As bad luck would have it, I bumped into the Chaplain from school on the road. Now, if it was anybody else caught sneaking out of school, they would have been dragged down to the principal's office by the ear and given a serious talking to. I looked him straight in the eye and said I was in town getting a present for my mother. He didn't even question me on it, that's part of me looking all sweet and innocent, I tend to get away with things that I shouldn't! I'm sure part of it is that people are afraid to upset me and also perhaps that they allow me to have some liberties as they know the struggles I have. Either way, I was able to enjoy some of the benefits of it over the years. I made a point of not taking advantage of it though, I still wanted to be treated in the same way as everyone else and I couldn't have expected that if I always got special treatment.

On a funny note, I've never once been asked for ID when going to a bar. I would just go ahead on in without really ever being questioned. I think there was a fear around asking me in case they caused offence but also a sense of them feeling uncomfortable with my disability. Back in the day there was a huge backlog in getting ID so we had to apply for a slip of paper from the Gardaí to prove we were over 18. One night a big 6ft tall bouncer was looking at this slip of paper and I just started arguing with him, at times my mouth really gets away with me. I think he thought it might be a fake piece of ID and I just lost it a bit. He told me I was really close to being brought down to the barracks with him but I just laughed and told him I would talk to him later. I don't think he wanted to push it anymore with me. I'm learning balance, is my point. I don't always have to shout to be heard, I don't want to come across as aggressive when what I mean to be is assertive.

Nursing homes. Oh boy...when I see nursing homes, I just see darkness. I just see being left alone. Nobody's going to bother with me. I just see tubes. I just see trying to be kept alive by machines. I've always said quality over quantity. Quality of life. It's extremely important to me. Quantity of life is important to me, of course, but I find it hard to see the quality in life if I am in a nursing home even though nursing homes nowadays are beautiful and the care provided is fantastic but I can't say it's for me. It's just for me, it feels like going to jail. My independence has been taken away from me.

'When it comes to aging, I think of the fact that my mom was told I will need 'around the clock' care.'They said to her that I'd never be able to walk and I would probably be brain damaged.

Those words do resound in my head, as I get older, and as I've become more dependent on services, or people, I suppose, again, I fought so hard for my independence, I'm damn not going to give it up for anybody.

I'm not saying I won't take support. Of course I will. But I can get support and still live in my own home, in my own comforts. Nowadays, so much is taken away from people with disabilities. A lot of people with disabilities can still live in their own homes, with a little support; extra support coming into them, whether it's morning or the night.

By offering this support you are giving the person with the disability their dignity by being in their own home around their own things. Just having that little independence - I think that's something that is taken away from people with disabilities far too soon.

CHAPTER 3

LIVING WITH DISABILITIES

You may be familiar with the Tony Robbins Power Stand.

it's a nonverbal expression of empowerment and strength. Strength within yourself standing tall. Even though I'm only four feet, I am standing tall and representing a strong woman in the disability community. This is extremely important to me.

It's also extremely important to me to look at society and how it sees people with disabilities.

Do we see them as people with strength? Or do we see them with weakness?

Do we see them with beauty? Beauty within beautiful the inside out? It gives a sense of curiousness.

Food for thought.

How do you actually see somebody with a disability?

In this photo, you can clearly see my deformity.

Throughout my life, I had been hiding my hypo scoliosis, but not anymore. I want this chapter to represent that you no longer have to hide. Stand tall and proud of who you are. I want this photo to represent that you can stand in your power. You no longer need to hide away from yourself, your peers, or society.

Stand in your power.

Be true to who you are. Show your vulnerabilities, but also show your strength.

Life as a woman with a disability can be very difficult. Women with disabilities often face discrimination and lower wages than able-bodied women, and they can also experience challenges such as inadequate access to healthcare and transportation. These factors can lead to difficulty in finding employment, maintaining relationships, and achieving financial stability. This is because of a lack of understanding of the unique needs of women with disabilities, as well as a lack of resources and support available to them. This can lead to feelings of isolation and a lack of self-confidence, both of which can further impede a woman with a disability from achieving her goals. 'This can be a difficult cycle to break. Without employment and financial stability, it can be harder to access resources that might help with self-confidence and building relationship.'

Additionally, there are often many barriers for women with disabilities, such as inaccessible workplaces and public spaces, which can further limit their opportunities. This can create a downward spiral where a woman with a disability may struggle to find employment.

Not having access to the resources necessary to build their skills and self-confidence can make it even harder to find and keep a job, leading to a lack of financial stability. This lack of financial stability can then lead to a lack of access to healthcare and other resources, creating a vicious cycle that can be difficult to break.

Furthermore, the additional discrimination faced by women with disabilities can limit their opportunities and make it challenging to find work. This can lead to a feeling of helplessness and lack of self-worth, making it even harder to break the cycle. Women with disabilities may also be more likely to face higher levels of poverty, and may have fewer opportunities to access education and other resources that can help them to build their skills and self-confidence. This combination of factors can lead to a widening of the gender and disability gaps, making it more difficult for women with disabilities to access the same opportunities as their non-disabled peers. As a result, they are more likely to be left behind in terms of job opportunities, education, and other resources that can provide them with a pathway to success and a sense of purpose. This is because many employers, educational institutions, and other organisations lack the particular accommodations and resources necessary to ensure that women with disabilities have the same access and opportunities as their non-disabled counterparts.

In addition, there may be a lack of awareness or understanding of the unique challenges that women with disabilities face, making it more difficult for them to be seen and heard. This can lead to barriers in employment, education, and other areas of life, as well as a feeling of invisibility and exclusion. As a result, women with disabilities often find themselves at a disadvantage when it comes to achieving their goals and finding success.

Additionally, these women may struggle to find role models or mentors who can help them navigate the world and advocate for themselves. This can make it difficult for them to gain the confidence and resources necessary to break the cycle of discrimination.

This can be particularly true in cases where women with disabilities are the only ones of their kind in the workplace or have limited access to support networks. This can lead to a lack of self-esteem, as they may not have the same opportunities as their peers and may feel as though they are not valued or respected. Moreover, this can lead to a sense of exclusion, as they may be left out of conversations and decisions, or not taken seriously.

Without support and acceptance, they may feel isolated and unheard, leading to further feelings of low self-esteem and self-worth. This can be especially damaging for women with disabilities, as their unique experience of intersectionality can be further compounded by the lack of recognition, understanding and acceptance from those around them. This can lead to feelings of powerlessness and disconnection from their peers and colleagues, further entrenching the exclusion they experience. Emphasising this, is essential to create a space of understanding and acceptance for women with disabilities, so they can develop a sense of belonging and empowerment within their communities. Fostering an inclusive environment is crucial in order to provide women with disabilities the opportunity to form meaningful connections, enabling them to feel empowered and accepted.

To achieve this, it is important to provide resources, access to education, and create a sense of community for women with disabilities. This will allow them to thrive and become an integral part of society. By doing this, we are sending a powerful message that everyone deserves equal rights, opportunities and recognition, regardless of their abilities.

Furthermore, by providing these resources, we are not only empowering women with disabilities, but also contributing to a more inclusive and equitable society. Additionally, we are providing a platform for them to share their stories and make their voices heard, creating a greater understanding and awareness of their needs. For instance, the platform can be used to share stories of successful women with disabilities who have been able to make a positive impact in their communities despite the challenges they face.

For example, one woman shared her story of how she was able to go back to school and graduate, despite having to deal with physical and mental health issues while studying. On the other hand, some people with disabilities feel that they are not being accurately represented by stories like these. They feel that these stories represent disabled women as being inspiring simply because they are able to do things that other people with disabilities are also able to do. There is no one-size-fits-all answer to whether or not disabled women are accurately represented in the media. It depends on the individual woman's story and how she chooses to tell it. It's like someone trying to explain to someone else what it's like to eat a mango. Everyone has a different experience, and it's difficult to accurately describe it without having the person try it for themselves. The same is true for disabled women and their experiences in the media; it's up to the individual to decide if they feel they are accurately represented.

In a survey, only 42% of disabled women said they feel that the facts of their identity that matter to them most are well-represented on screen. In a survey cited on prnewswire.com, 70% of women said they still don't feel represented in the images they see every day.

I'm often asked what it is like having a disability or even several disabilities. Well, I can tell you that it can be a serious daily challenge trying to navigate through a world that wasn't designed to be accessible to everyone, especially when you have a disability. Having to ask for help can be a really difficult thing to do especially if you are as independent, as I am, many people who know me might use the word 'stubborn' and sometimes, to be truthful, it can be hard to maintain a positive attitude when faced with ignorance or discrimination.

But at the same time, it has also taught me resilience and patience, and I'm more appreciative of the little things in my life. As such, I've come to recognise that accessibility challenges can be seen not only as obstacles, but also as opportunities to grow and learn and I bring this into my coaching with people.

I've learned to be more patient with others, to think through problems and solutions in a different way than I might have just five years ago, and to recognise the importance of speaking up when something isn't working. And oh, how I have learned that particular one!

However, there are also challenges that come with living with a disability. For example, I have to be super careful about planning my day-to-day activities, because I never know when I might need to adjust my plans. I also have to be mindful of how my disability might affect others and be sure to communicate my needs clearly.

This is similar to navigating a stormy sea, as you have to be flexible and prepared for whatever challenges come your way, while also being conscious of how your actions might impact your crewmates. As Socrates once said: "Be kind, for everyone you meet is fighting a hard battle."

CHAPTER 4

RELATIONSHIPS

It took me a long time to realise that the most important relationship was with oneself. That sets the tone for every other relationship in your life. This photo represents relationships in my life. It represents that I have become present with my soul and realising I am not my shell. I am so much more and so are you. I've taken the time to get to know me, from the inside out. It has been scary getting to know the real me as some people don't know the real story behind the smile. Now's the time that I have chosen to step out of my own darkness and into the light. I would like to spend my life or share my life with somebody else. It also represents a sense of protection. For me, protecting myself has been one of the most important things to me in a relationship. I have been hurt many times in the past, as all of us have.

They say with each hurt you learn a lesson, which is true. However for me I feel the hurt had closed me up. It felt scary to show that part of me as I am always seen as the warrior. Becoming vulnerable is very difficult. It always has been, even when I say the word vulnerable, it's kind of scary. That one person knowing you from inside out, knowing the good things, the bad things and your quirks. The picture also represents a sense of softness, because I feel like this in society. Sometimes I am seen as a tough cookie. This photo represents my soft and gentle side and this picture also represents surrendering. Surrendering to oneself, and accepting myself for who I am. And surrendering myself to another person. Being vulnerable in the presence of somebody else. Letting that person know my soul and letting myself be vulnerable with that person. Even though it sounds scary, I believe it is time in my life. I can take this step and this is what this photo represents to me, even though it is scary. By me learning to be vulnerable, it is giving me the opportunity to grow as a human being and build a deeper connection with myself and others. When I look at this picture I see a soul and not just a shell.

Relationships. Ooh, that's a biggie. Relationships provide us with companionship and support, which can help us deal with difficult situations. And, in our lifetimes, we are all going to experience difficult situations. We are all going to be 'let down' and disappointed by others. That's just how life goes.

Relationships also teach us valuable skills such as communication, empathy, and compromise, which can be applied in many different areas of life. In addition, having someone to rely on in times of distress can help us to stay calm and rational, rather than making rash decisions that we may later regret. Haven't we all done that? At least once?

Having a healthy relationship can also give us a sense of security, allowing us to focus on our goals and dreams. This ultimately leads to a sense of fulfillment, as we are able to accomplish more when we have a supportive family member, friend or partner to lean on. Furthermore, there's loads of research that asserts that having a stable relationship, in which we can trust the other person to be there for us, can provide us with a greater sense of self-worth, allowing us to strive towards our aspirations with confidence.

As we are supported in relationships and we work together to reach our goals, the feeling of accomplishment and satisfaction leads to a greater sense of mutual achievement. Additionally, having a reliable person or people that we can trust and rely on gives us the assurance and reassurance that we need to feel secure in ourselves and our decisions. This, in turn, helps us to focus more on our ambitions and take action towards achieving them.

On the other hand, a negative relationship with 'self' can really hold us back in life. A negative relationship with self means having a poor opinion of oneself, which can lead to low self-esteem and a lack of confidence, which can then prevent us from achieving our goals in life. It can stop us living day to day. It can make us miserable.

Low self-esteem can make it difficult to take risks, try new things, or even put ourselves out there to meet other people and do new things to take us out of the boring everyday life. We may be too afraid to speak up, ask for help, or take on challenging tasks and this is particularly destructive for anyone with disabilities.

Consequently, we miss out on opportunities to grow, learn, and succeed and, as a result, we often don't reach our full potential, and our negative relationship with ourselves can have lasting consequences. For example, research shows that people with low self-esteem are more likely to experience depression, anxiety, and other mental health issues, as well as difficulties in their relationships and lower overall life satisfaction. People with low self-esteem are more likely to engage in self-destructive behaviours such as substance abuse, self-harm, and disordered eating.

Low self-esteem is like a poisonous fog that clouds one's perspective and affects every area of their life. It can be hard to break free from, but it is possible with the help of a supportive network of family and friends.

Sense of self, or self-consciousness, is the awareness you have of your own thoughts, feelings, and physical sensations. It's what allows you to know that you are a separate and unique individual. Self-consciousness is a powerful concept that allows you to recognise and appreciate your individual identity. Self-consciousness gives you the ability to recognise and express your own opinion, values, beliefs, and make individual decisions based on what is important to you. For example, self-consciousness allows you to know when you are feeling an emotion and to take the necessary steps to manage it. Really, self-consciousness is like a fingerprint, unique and individual to each person, and is something that can never be duplicated. Only 10 to 15 percent of people fit the criteria for being self-conscious, according to some estimates (source: betterup.com).

Beginning any relationship for me was always going to be a bit different from the experience of someone without my conditions. I knew that from a young age, but I was determined not to let it stop me. I felt very strongly that I deserved the same love and support as anyone else and although I knew I might face challenges that others wouldn't, I still wanted to share my life with another person. My heart and soul are the same as yours, even though my body is not. However, with the question of relationships, comes the question of sex. How would that be for me, I wondered? Would there be anyone who could see past my body? In fact I wondered would there be anyone who could see my body as a beautiful part of me rather than need to see past it?

I'm actually a shy person, I do consider myself kind of reserved by nature and I do find it hard maybe sometimes to let down my walls in order to get to know people. I have gotten a lot better as the years have gone by, but I do believe that's maturity and that's to learning experiences and being more open to learning as time goes on.

I come from a country background where everything is so quiet and everything is so private and so reserved and that if you were seeking to do anything out of the ordinary it was considered crazy. Disabled people are portrayed in society as ones who should just stay in the corner and not be seen or heard. I did carry that with me throughout my youth and it's been hard to shake off. I've grown up with the element of people pleasing and I didn't care how I felt inside as long as I was seen in a good light. I think it was expected of me not to thrive too much and not to entertain the idea of a perfect loving relationship.

Relationships in general were more difficult for me, I was okay if they didn't go deeper than the surface, but once they did, I'd always put my disability to the forefront of it. I would name it and say I have scoliosis and list all the things wrong with me. Then when they ran for the hills as some did, I wasn't surprised. I wasn't putting all the good things about me out there, so I think I set myself up for a few falls, I just didn't want to risk rejection too often and it felt easier to protect myself.

I never wanted to be seen as a disabled woman because I always grew up in mainstream society. So, I wanted to be seen as a part of mainstream society, and not to be seen as some kind of tourist attraction. I know people get really curious about disabled people and sex, and I'm generally happy to answer their questions, but sometimes it felt like people just assumed I should be asexual and not have the same desires as anyone else. I set myself up for a fall when I started to say eventually that I didn't see myself with someone who had a disability, I just felt I had so much wrong with me already that I didn't want someone who couldn't support me when I needed it. I guess my family thought I would end up getting hurt and that I should 'stick to my own' in case someone came along who just wanted to use me.

A disabled person could have wanted to use me too, but somehow that wasn't addressed. When that perception was presented to me, I rebelled a bit and decided to go in the opposite direction, I didn't feel I should only have to date disabled people just because I am disabled.

There are two versions of me sometimes, the public persona Siobhán and the private one. There are some similarities of course but I don't always show my pain to the outside world, I don't want to always be out there crying. There is a soft side to me, and I have a large heart but I'm still a work in progress, like everyone else. The thing with relationships is that most people get to start exploring them in school, that's a missing piece of the puzzle for me because that didn't happen in my life.

I am just learning as I go along. It's like the blind leading the blind, I don't know what I'm at. When it comes to relationships or friendships, sometimes, I'm doing the best I can. Take motherhood for example. You're not just handed a child with an instruction manual and told how to do it. I feel like that within society as well. I'm literally just trying to figure out things as I go along. And sometimes I've made the most whopper of mistakes. But I am a firm believer that we have to make these mistakes in order to learn and I have learned so much from my mistakes. I've been in friendships and relationships that haven't been any good for me at all, in any way, shape or form.

But in a strange way, I am thankful for those because I can now see the red flags. Many times in the past there would have been big flashing red lights and I would have ignored them and got caught up in all the drama. I think I'm very thankful now that I've had that learning experience because as I get older, I just don't want to waste the time, I need a deeper connection.

Nowadays I think the whole dating scene is difficult because a lot of it is online. I'm jealous of my parents' generation when they would just go to a dance and meet someone with no fuss. They might only talk once a week and there was no worry about being ghosted or judged by one picture on Tinder. So, it's harder, especially for someone in my position, so I shy away from it. A lot of the time when I was younger, I just assumed boys wouldn't be into me anyway because of my disability and I always did push that to the front. I just didn't want to get hurt, so I was protecting myself. I did have crushes though, plenty of them, but I labelled myself as a girl with a disability and rejection was a huge fear of mine.

Me having relationships was never spoken about in the family home because obviously, the focus was for me was to stay well, and to keep me as well as possible and keep me out of hospital, more so than anything else, health was the main focus. The older I got, the more scared I was to explore relationships because I was trying to protect myself from rejection. I think that's a massive thing for somebody with a disability. The thought of being rejected was devastating for me, especially when I was younger. I wouldn't have had the emotional maturity or development to be able to cope with it. I suppose for that reason I never put myself out there too much and I never had a massive group of friends.

Sex education wasn't a thing in my house, mum never really sat down and told me about the birds and bees. The only thing she would ever say was 'just be careful'. Maybe it was assumed I didn't need the talk because my shell was so different that it wouldn't be an option for me. I'm still figuring it all out, I was pretty clueless and would talk to my friends about it to try and learn. I did always feel like I was still a woman with my own desires, I need to know about this stuff. The first time I ever had a conversation about contraception was with my gynaecologist. I think over the years mum has learned to be more open with me about it, she's had to be because I need to talk about it, why shouldn't I?

Sometimes I feel as if society has tried to scare us into not having sex, as if somehow it's bad or a sin. I don't understand that, we might have bodies that look different and function a little differently than someone without a disability, but we still desire the same things. We still need and deserve to be loved and desired. The risk of rejection for me is much higher than it is for someone without my disability and that really gets me down sometimes, it's hard to take. That's why I feel it's really important to discuss sex education in the same way it would be with anyone, disabled or not. That way, we can teach society that we have the same thoughts, feelings and needs as anyone else, we can normalise it.

Sex education in schools is different for people with disabilities. It's taught at a later stage, which doesn't make sense to me. There's no justification for that in my opinion, we have the same rights to learn about it as able-bodied people. I've also come to learn that the information we are given is often a softer version of the standard mainstream stuff. I think that needs to change and I will voice that over and over again. There were many days that I felt I couldn't talk about sex or ask questions because of my condition, that somehow I wasn't supposed to go down that road or that nobody would want to with me anyway.

It's heart-breaking, because inside me I'm still feeling like every girl out there when it comes to sex but on the outside I was supposed to pretend it didn't factor into my life.

When I did start to put myself 'out there', it started with just opening my mind to the idea of a relationship, I didn't even begin to put myself out there physically for a while. I thought I should maybe start with letting my walls down just a bit first. Then I would go out for a night and just tell myself I would see how it goes, without any plan. I just allowed myself to experience. When anybody would talk to me, it felt like unknown territory. Back then I would beat myself up for things that I said, thinking I sounded stupid. I came to see that maybe it was just me stopping myself, people did talk to me and it helped me get over the extreme anxiety I had about it. I still have a fear to this day that someone will be embarrassed to be seen in public with me and want to keep our relationship a secret.

The idea of being rejected for something that I just have no control or power over is pretty hard to manage. I have no power over it. It's not as if I was being rejected for something I could change, like not being a nice person. I simply can't change the way I look. I think it's just another one of the things that I've never spoken about in public that much. The feeling in the family home too was that I'd be better off being independent without risking rejection or having to answer to anyone. I think it was down to my family feeling both afraid and uncomfortable for me, they didn't really want to speak about it too much. My mum really doesn't understand dating in todays' world where people hook up and say 'good luck' the next morning on their way out the door. It's alien to her. So I really only speak about this kind of stuff on a surface level with family, I don't see the point in going any deeper.

I did meet someone once who was not afraid at all to be seen with me, it didn't have to be behind closed doors. I'm so glad that was one of my first experiences because they were proud to be with me and hold my hand. That meant a lot to me, I find hand holding really comforting anyway so it really helped my confidence and showed me I can be attractive too. He liked me, for me. Although the relationship didn't last, I found that being liked for who I was, and I mean for ALL of who I was, set a tone for me. It enabled me to start off in the relationship world on the right foot, knowing how it felt to be truly seen and accepted. It gave me a good idea of what it feels like to be in a healthy relationship. I'm just like anyone else, I want to be seen and heard and loved. Feeling that I deserved that to the same degree as anyone else was a journey for me. I knew in my heart that I was just as deserving as everyone else, but I wasn't sure if other people would see that.

Sadly, we do tend to judge people by their appearance and mine is quite different to people without my conditions. I had to be very aware that not everyone would be able to see past it and choose to involve myself only with those people who could love all of me. I might not always have known who that was in advance, but it became apparent pretty quickly.

I have gone through phases in my life where I only saw the stereotypical woman as beautiful, it has taken me years to get to the place where all women are beautiful no matter what ailment, shape, size, colour they are, it doesn't matter. We're all beautiful. But again, that's not something that I've learned overnight, I'm a firm believer that you just don't switch off your mindset, you work on your mindset. it takes time to acknowledge the fact that, yes, I do have these quirks and I want to iron them out. It took me years of pushing through fears to put myself out there a bit more. Sometimes I was knocked down and sometimes I wasn't. It's been a very long journey of learning to love who I am and how my body is. There were times I cried myself to sleep because I had been rejected or things hadn't turned out like I'd hoped. I spent plenty of time protecting myself and being guarded after something had hurt me. I was scared of taking risks again, there's only so much rejection and fight one can take. There were days when I let it all get on top of me and I'd let myself sit in the sadness of that for a long time.

Eventually, outright stubbornness and determination would shine through and I'd get myself up out of my bed, shake myself off and try to find a way forward. I want to live life to the fullest, despite how hard that can be for me a lot of the time, and relationships are part of that. So, me being me, I'd bounce back with my humour intact and my heart all the wiser. I refused to give up and succumb to what I thought society wanted me to be.

There are a few times I've been rejected that have shaped me as a person today. A huge one for me was when I did have a partner, but I felt he was ashamed to be seen with me in public. We didn't go anywhere publicly, not to the cinema or out for a meal. I tried to fool myself that I was ok with that, actually I got to the stage where I was just grateful for his company, and that's not a good place to be in. I put my desires aside and thought I should just be happy with it. The truth was I felt a deep rejection of who I was as a person, I really had to step back and put myself first. I discovered I really wanted and deserved someone who had no shame about being seen with me. That was a big step forward for me and a really important lesson in my self-worth.

Quite possibly the most important one for me was when I was in a relationship with someone who really did love me. Similar to the relationship I talked about earlier, he wasn't afraid of being seen in public with me, he held my hand when we went to a restaurant or the cinema. I was on cloud nine, I thought all my Christmases had come at once. After a while though, I got that feeling that something wasn't quite right, I noticed a distance between us. Us women know, we know when something starts to change. Then, I got the dreaded text saying, 'we need to talk'. My stomach sank in that moment, I thought things had been a bit off but didn't expect that text.

He ended it with me because I can't have children, and he really wanted children of his own. I had been honest with him about that issue from the start, but I can only guess that as time went on, it bothered him more and more. I couldn't even be angry with him about it, he was honest and simply had the natural desire to have children one day. I will never forget how my whole world seemed to shatter right in front of my eyes. I was completely devastated. It took me a very long time to come to terms with that. In the end, I thank him, he helped me to see that I was still depending on a relationship to feel accepted and loved, but what a hard journey that was!

It's important for me to talk about children. Of course, I wish I could have them, but I can't. It's something that has taken me a lot of inner work to come to terms with. Ladies, we all know that giving the gift of life is one of the most beautiful things we can ever give someone and it's the one thing I'm not able to give. The romantic rejection of me because of this, was devastating. Not enough people talk about how hard it is for someone in my position to come to terms with not being able to conceive. Why shouldn't we want to be mothers? All too often, it's simply assumed that we don't want to, or shouldn't want to, and I don't think there's enough support out there for it. I would love to be able to have children, it hasn't been easy for me to accept that it's simply something that won't happen for me and I do know that any partner I go on to have will need to be someone who knows that, and is as ok with it as possible.

The question of pregnancy for someone with disabilities is a massive point of interest. Not everyone with a disability will be able to have children, although many can. It's a very individual thing and depends solely on the specific conditions and how possible and safe a pregnancy might be for them. While that sounds straightforward, it isn't. It doesn't take into account that it can be absolutely devastating to hear that you can't carry a child.

It's devastating for anyone to hear that they can't fulfil that dream and the natural desire to pro-create. It's something I don't think is talked about enough when it comes to women with disabilities. It can lead to depression, low-esteem, anger, despair and another level of rejection. It can also make it hard, as it did in my case, to form a long-standing relationship with someone who does want to have children. That issue is a whole other level of acceptance of limitations that people with disabilities are faced with accepting. As if we don't have enough to deal with already. It's heart-breaking, it really is.

I think my whole life has been so focused on looking after myself and dealing with my own medical condition, that I would relish the chance to nurture someone else. I feel I have a lot of love in my heart to share and a child would be the perfect person to do it with. It's an ongoing process for me to accept that I can't have that. I'm lucky that now I do have an adorable niece. She has been a light in my life, and many other people's lives, but more on her later.

I'm 36 and I'm still learning to drive when it comes to relationships, because I've really only been dating since I turned 29 years old. That's only 6 years' experience. I'm trying to have more compassion and kindness for myself when it comes to learning about the dating world. I still struggle with my worthiness, my shell isn't stereotypically beautiful, I don't have the curves, I don't have a womanly figure, but I do have a cracking personality. It's a bold thing to say but some men do want to date people with a disability, some for the right reasons, but there are some who want to do it to be seen as a hero. So, it's not easy for me to trust when a guy says he likes me. I don't want or need to be minded; I don't need a partner. I want one. That's two different things.

When I started to put myself out there, I had to realise that I was putting up with more than I should have because I felt it was all I deserved or that he was acting badly because of me and my disability. I came to a sharp realisation that sometimes people just behave badly and it's nothing to do with me. Sometimes I cut people off straightaway by telling them upfront about my disability when I thought I was just being honest, it came across as putting my scoliosis up front and centre instead of who I am as a person. That has been a major learning curve for me, I realised that if all I did was identify myself by my disability, then that's what potential partners would do too. I had to learn to value who I am as a person, not regardless of my body but inclusive of my body.

I will generally talk to someone online for a few weeks and see if there's a connection, if there is we can go for a coffee. I'm not going to get all dressed up to the nines with full make up for that. Anybody can take a good photo these days with all the filters involved, I would much rather just meet someone and see what we think of each other. I have a lot of respect for someone who doesn't waste my time and build up a connection with me for months before saying they can't cope with it anymore. I'd rather someone be honest on the first date if we know it's not going to go anywhere. I don't want emotions tampered with on either side.

I think the attraction for boys has kind of always been there, I'm the same as any other female on the planet. When it comes to relationships, with all the medical stuff I've had going on, I never really considered it much of an option for me because my focus was so much on staying well and getting better all the time. My energy was taken up with making sure I was strong and healthy to the best of my ability, and time just seemed to pass by so quickly. Our teenage years are the most impressionable, the most important years of our life because that's where our learning experiences come from, we're learning about ourselves, our set beliefs are formed after the age of seven. So up until the age of seven, we believe everything that is taught to us by our parents and whatever their beliefs are. But after the age of seven, we started to get more curious and develop our own set of beliefs. But I don't think for me, I developed my own set of beliefs until later in life.

I was quite old fashioned when it came to my ideas about relationships, I always thought I was born in the wrong time. I assumed you just found your 'person', there was no running around kissing lots of frogs to find prince charming. I suppose it was a simple way of looking at it, as if you just found them and got married and that was that. Sadly, that's not the truth. When I realised that I went into a different mode, one of thinking I had to work really hard in a relationship and not letting it all come naturally. There was something in me at one stage where I felt I really needed to be seen in a relationship, to be accepted by society and to show that I was loved by someone. As I've come to love myself more, I don't need that outside validation anymore. I don't need to beg someone to spend time with me or put myself in situations that compromise my self-worth anymore.

Learning what relationships are for me has been my biggest teacher, firstly my relationship with myself, as I mentioned at the beginning of this chapter. And secondly, my relationship with the opposite sex. Every relationship I have is showing me how to learn to love myself on a much deeper level. Every time I'm rejected, I'm learning. And every time I'm accepted for who I am, I'm learning more and more about love.

CHAPTER 5

SOCIAL MEDIA AND ME

This Picture represents social media and me. We live in a generation where social media has taken over, you have Tik Tok, you have Instagram, you have Facebook, Every App, you name it, we are contactable and available at any given time. Even though social media has had a positive impact on many areas of our lives, it has also had a downside in terms of the negative impact it can have on people. Social media can lead to sadness because each and every single one of us do not know what is really going on for anyone on the inside, or what's going on for them behind closed doors.

In recent years, you will have heard the hashtag 'Be Kind' but I wonder are people actually being kind, or they just saying words and not putting them into action?

Sometimes I wonder.......

The fear in the eyes indicates vulnerability, and not being able to show who that person truly is in fear of being judged or being laughed at. Being different in today's society is very difficult.

And social media hasn't been easy as it doesn't advocate widely for people with differences. Sometimes it gives an opportunity for them to be laughed at.

I do see a change in today's social media, which is very much welcomed. It'll take time. But over time, I do believe social media will become a place of authenticity, a place where we can truly be ourselves.

A place where we won't have to just be advertising our good days and that we can come on and talk about the bad days. Because I don't know about you. But those people are the people that inspire me. Those are the people that I can relate to, real people, authentic people, people just like you and I.

It's okay to be scared. This photo, it represents being scared, being scared to show who you really are. But over time I have learned that it's okay to be who I am. The Good, the Bad and the quirky sometimes. We're all just human beings doing the very best we can.

Before I tell you all this story…girls we have all done it and even the lads too whether or not you want to admit it. About two years ago, I went to through a tough relationship break up and all the usual emotions happened. I found myself gravitating towards social media to see how he was doing. Yes, I know now that it was an unhealthy trait. When I would see him on social media looking like he was having the time of his life, I found myself getting angry saying things like, "this is so fucking unfair I am here lying in bed crying my heart out while he is out there smiling having a great time". You see, social media is designed to show the best of us not the worst. I guess what I'm trying to say is I was mindreading the situation. Mind reading is a habitual thinking pattern characterised by expecting others to know what you are thinking without having to tell them or expecting to know what others are thinking without them telling you. You never really know truly what's going on inside someone's four walls or head.

Alright, let's talk about social media and how it has become a huge part of our lives in the western world. I mean, who would have thought that platforms like Facebook, Instagram, Twitter, and TikTok would have such a big impact on our daily routines, right? But they do. Oh, and they, or whatever they soon morph into are here to stay.

It's crazy to think about, but social media has become a staple in the lives of millions of people. From scrolling through our feeds first thing in the morning to using it as a way to unwind before bed, it's safe to say that social media is pretty much everywhere. And let's not forget about how it's become a tool for businesses to market their products, as well as a way for people to stay connected with friends and family, even if they're on the other side of the world. Don't worry, I'm not on a hard sell here. I'm just stating the facts. But how did social media become so ubiquitous? Well, it all started with the creation of platforms like Myspace and Facebook, which were initially meant to connect people within a specific community. But as these platforms grew in popularity, they began to offer more features, such as the ability to share photos, videos, and posts, which made them even more appealing to users. Everywhere!

And then came along platforms like ones I love to use myself such as Instagram and Twitter, which allowed users to share even more personal aspects of their lives, like their thoughts and experiences. And let's not forget about TikTok, which has become a cultural phenomenon, particularly among younger generations. Yeah, yeah, I'm not that old! And, you might find me on it yet.

One of the things I've noticed is that the biggest appeal of social media is the instant gratification it provides and this is now a major research area in psychology. Social media offers a quick fix and is the distraction of all distractions as we endlessly scroll through other people's supposedly wonderful lives.

And with everything in life, with the good, comes the bad. Social media can, and very often is, a major source of negativity and drama, with people using it to harass and bully others – both subtly and overtly. And let's not forget about the potential for misinformation/disinformation etc., as well as the negative impact it can have on our mental health, with many people feeling so overwhelmed by the constant need to stay connected and up-to-date. I'm one of those people!

It seems to me that there is a real lack of accurate representation of adult female disability issues across all the various social media platforms (I don't need to name names but you know who you are!). Research by the Pew Research Center, as just one example, found that only 18% of Americans say they have a 'good' understanding (I know, I know, that's pretty vague but does give a sense of what's going on) of what living with a physical disability is like. I really believe this lack of awareness contributes significantly to the overall stigma and stereotyped ideas that all too many people living with disabilities face every day.

It's quite unbelievable, but a recent study published by disability charity, Scope, found that just one percent of social media posts about disability (in any context!) were from women. This disproportionately low representation of female voices across social media surely has a negative impact on how we all perceive the lives of women with disabilities, and in turn, impacts on how we, as a society, might value the rights of disabled women. This issue has been emphasised by a recent Twitter campaign to highlight the lack of female representation in the media and to raise awareness of the need for better representation of disabled people in general.

The hashtag #WomenInPublicLife has already gained over 11,000 tweets, and has been widely shared across social media platforms.

One of the most significant barriers to wider representation in social media is the lack of diverse perspectives of people with disabilities. There are many individuals and groups whose views are simply not being adequately reflected in mainstream publications and social media, simply because these individuals are not given the opportunity to speak in the first instance. Changing this mindset can be difficult, however, it is more important than ever to ensure all voices are heard. If ignored, those groups will continue to face discrimination, and their rights to equal understanding and treatment will remain unfulfilled. While we have made progress in recent years in improving representation of marginalised communities in the media, there is still a long way to go before minority groups are truly represented at all levels of society.

And this is particularly the case for people with disabilities across social media. In modern society, having a successful career is very important for many people and can provide them with the financial independence that they need to support themselves and their families.

Unfortunately, many people with physical disabilities are hindered in their attempts to reach this goal. One of the main reasons for this is the fact that, unfortunately, our society isn't very accepting of people with disabilities more generally. Is it fair to say that it pretends to be; that it sets out to be so. But it just isn't.

This attitude is often reflected in the way people with a disability in the workplace are represented across social media. What's ironic in all of this is that inclusiveness and diversity are central to the ethos of most social and professional organisations, so it is disappointing to see that there is still such a long way to go in terms of equality in the workplace and how this is discussed on media.

A recent study conducted by Mercer found that almost a third (32%) of all global employers believe that they have a 'critical' problem with gender balance within their organisation. The survey revealed, as an example, that this issue is particularly acute in the technology sector, with 61% of respondents indicating that a lack of female talent was either "a critical" or "high priority" issue for them.

Additionally, there is a disturbing and growing trend of social media users discussing female disabilities in what may be considered to be an unprofessional and insensitive manner. Some users seem to post pictures of themselves with supposed disabilities in a joking or mocking manner, often using derogatory language which causes confusion and hurt. Many people who identify as disabled use social media to share their unique experiences, including photographs of themselves and their life with a disability. I am one of those people and this book is testimony to that! Trends that concern me include not only the use of derogatory language, but also posts that demean the lived experience of having a disability and posts that set out to encourage others not to associate with people with disabilities!

For example, some accounts display pornographic images depicting people with disabilities in degrading and insulting ways. This type of content can cause extreme hurt to people living with disabilities by damaging their self-esteem and encouraging negative attitudes towards people who are disabled.

It is important to note that not all posts of this type are intended to be harmful and may be the result of ignorance on the part of the poster rather than a malicious intent to belittle people with disabilities. However, it can be hurtful for people with disabilities to see this type of content and can lead to them feeling isolated and unsupported by people online. And remember, the online world is where we all now spend so much of our time. For many, it is their reality.

While it is important to call out offensive behaviour when we see it, we should remember that the person behind the account may have a disability and therefore may not have control over what they share online or how they choose to present themselves online. It is also important to remember that many people with disabilities use social media to connect with others and find support, so respect and support of each other online are to be encouraged.

I find the best way to combat such negative representation is to raise our own awareness of these issues and educate ourselves about the struggles of living with a disability. By being thoughtful and respectful in our online interactions we can eliminate stigma.

What exactly am I talking about? Some examples of what I deem to be inappropriate content include: posts encouraging violence against people with a physical disability; use of offensive terms to describe people who have a mental illness; and pictures of people in wheelchairs with captions such as "Wouldn't it be funny if..." or "I wish I was...". Examples of acceptable posts include: positive messages about someone's disability; posts sharing ideas on how to live well with a disability; or positive portrayals of people with disabilities in the media or popular culture.

So, on the plus side, social media has allowed people with a whole range of hidden and obvious disabilities to, themselves, create and share content that helpfully counteracts the negative stereotypes associated with their disability. By providing a positive narrative about their lives, these people are helping to change the public's perception of what it means to be disabled. And I am in this category.

With all that being said, I find social media really interesting. It's hard to imagine what life was like before it.

It has opened my life up in ways that I would have struggled to do without it. Most of it in good ways but at times, I have been exposed to the darker side of it. That's always a risk, no matter who you are, when you put yourself out there online. I have seen the many benefits it brings in connecting with people but sadly, I've also seen how hurtful comments can destroy your confidence for a while. I think we need more education for the younger generation on how to use social media responsibly. Not only for the younger ones, but for anyone really. People need to be made aware of the impact of their words and for there to be more accountability when it comes to what you say and what you share. I don't think being able to set up fake accounts with fake names should ever be allowed.

It only leads to people being able to do and say whatever they like with no consequences. There are some changes coming in recently in relation to this. I've noticed more talks on the topic in schools and campaigns online to promote online kindness, but it still isn't enough. We need more of that; we need more control over the content that can be posted and monitoring of the comments that people can write. It's devastating to read about younger people who have harmed themselves or taken their own lives due to online bullying. This has to stop. Part of my mission is to raise as much awareness of this as possible, not just for people with disabilities, but for everyone.

I use social media differently now that I have matured somewhat. I am able to meet people from all over the world, to network and set up connections with others. These are people whom I would never have met in person in my day-to-day life. With having a small business now, I'm much more able to connect with people who have a similar mindset to me. Now I'm in my later 30's, social media is more of a way to connect with people than it was in my 20's. For me it was more about image then, the latest outfit or trend. Now, it's about how I can use it to help and support others. I want to read about people's journeys and what they have been through. I can use social media to share my story too. I like it when social media can be a realistic place to hang out in, where people are sharing ups and downs and their bad days along with their good ones.

In my 20's I would have put up posts partly to get likes, it would have given me an adrenalin rush that didn't last long. Now I'm in my 30's, my adrenalin rush comes from knowing I'm helping people, that I have made a difference to someone. I know my boundaries now; I know what's good for me and what isn't.

I feel a lot more confident and in control of what I share and I don't respond so emotionally to any negative feedback I might get.

I always want to use social media as a safe place. I think it's got such a stigma of badness and bullying these days. I always intend to use social media as a place to lift people up and to spread positivity. And I still want to do that. But I think since Covid-19 I'm a bit more open. I'm a very positive person and that will still come across in the messages that I deliver on social media. These days I have more of a happy medium, I'm more realistic. I can post about getting up in the morning and not feeling 100%. Before, I felt that I always have to tell the world I'm feeling fantastic, everything's wonderful and that there's no negativity going on in my world. I can kind of post now that I am having a bad day but that I know it's not going to last forever. That's more of a realistic way of looking at it. And I'm not so afraid of the backlash. I've had to change my perception of it quite a bit.

I found out the hard way that there can be quite instant negative backlash. Some years ago, I did a live video about living with kidney failure, but I got a number of comments about how I didn't know what I was talking about, because I wasn't a medical professional. That was hard to take for a few different reasons. Firstly, I was really putting myself and my body health out there for public knowledge, I was hoping for support in some form or another. And, I was hoping that my post might inspire or help someone else. That was my intention. I wasn't expecting negative comments like that, I wasn't prepared for how it would make me feel.

I have never said in any shape or form, that I am a doctor or a nurse or anything of that calibre. I did get backlash from people saying that I didn't comment enough on my doctors and nurses. I admire the doctors and nurses and the medical professionals in Ireland and it was really hard to get negative feedback online about me simply talking about my own experiences. I started to think that if one person said something negative, then everyone must be thinking the same and that I should just shut up.

I suppose for want of a better word; it frightened the life out of me. I was really proud of my live videos, and I did get a lot of positive feedback. All it took was for one person to come out of the woodwork and say something nasty and I removed my video. It was disappointing really, we're all human and I just wanted to talk and give my perspective. I think I was disappointed with myself more, for not standing up for myself.

It's amazing the influence that one person on social media can have if we take on their opinion. That was a huge learning curve for me. I've learned that we all have different maps of the world and those people who post negative comments probably have stuff of their own going on. It's definitely made me more passionate about mental health, so I think today I'm more truthful online, I don't stay middle of the road or sit on any fences, but I do keep other's feelings in mind too, I don't want to trigger anyone.

At the time, that whole thing made me feel that I ought to just be quiet and not talk about it at all. Over time though, I learned to just share my own opinions and perspectives and people can take it or leave it. I try not to take the comments personally and just hope that my posts reach someone who might need them.

When it comes to how people with disabilities are portrayed and received on social media, I think there's a long way to go yet. I find people are amazed that I can tie my own shoelaces just because I'm disabled. I think social media can be a bit patronising towards people who are disabled, we can still work, we can still set up businesses, we can still live our lives. I think it falls short. I say that because I can see there's a fear around people interacting with those online with disabilities. The fear seems to be around not knowing what to say, in case of saying something wrong and causing offence. So, it ends up that very little is said about disabilities as people feel it's better to say nothing than to get it wrong.

I don't think our voices are coming to the forefront enough at all yet. So little is discussed about the ways in which we suffer or the things that we might need. We have voices and they deserve to be heard in relation to our hopes and dreams and the support that we can both offer to others and ask from others. In my opinion, just because something is difficult to talk about, it doesn't mean we shouldn't try or be given the platform to try at least.

I am noticing an upward trend of disabilities being represented on TV programmes, which I'm happy about. I'm not sure how much of it is actually progressive or if it's just tokenism, but either way, it's putting in people's faces at home, so that's something positive. At the very least I would hope it would encourage people to see those with disabilities as people with hopes and dreams like them, maybe a bit different in their abilities, but the same at heart. I'm still a bit on the fence as to whether it's actually being done for the right reasons, but at least it's bringing it forward somewhat. I'm not sure how authentic it is, as there's very little talk about the challenges that we face.

It could simply be that people with disabilities are being included on TV and radio because they have to tick boxes to show they are inclusive.

I think it's still lacking in real representation, but it's a start. I think we are still put into boxes and labelled, when on TV for example, if the person on screen is the only one with a disability, they will stick out like a sore thumb. They are still lower in the hierarchy that nobody really wants to admit still exists. It's rare to see a disabled person on a TV show being married with 3 children. It's almost as though they think we are incapable of that.

The topic of how we might have babies seems to be taboo, as if people don't know how we would ever get pregnant and where we would put the babies in our body.

Over the years I have befriended social media more and more. I like posting and sharing videos about my journey and the experiences I have had. I am a lot more comfortable now showing people when I am going through a rough time. I believe it's important to talk about it all, not just about positive and happy aspects. The purpose of doing all that is to show others that it's ok not to be ok at times and to know we all feel the same sometimes. I think I'm sharing my experience so that people will know what they are feeling is normal. I like to think that I'm teaching and supporting people through their emotions, to help them see it's ok to feel happy, sad and angry.

I guess I'm still treading lightly after my experience of being trolled. But I am more open. I will go on social media now if my hair isn't even brushed whereas before I'd have to go on full hair and makeup. Everything had to be perfect. So now I'm little bit more authentic with who I am.

And then I am acknowledging how I'm feeling but as I always say, I never unpack there. I don't want the world to know everything I feel all the time, I suppose I'm still protective of some of the deeper emotions I have. We can all have a little bit of a protective layer and I do believe it's a healthy thing to have.

I see my role in social media now is to just be as authentic as possible. These days if you don't have 10,000 followers, you're 'nobody'. But I don't need that, I might just come home one day and have a few words of wisdom that I want to share. If people can take something from it, that's great. If they can't, that's ok too. I'm very intentional with my words on social media so I don't even comment on my own posts very often and I certainly don't waffle on Instagram about what I've eaten for breakfast. I'm not sure who would want to hear that anyway. We all know what food looks like. I just want to give a few inspirational words now and again and encourage others to see people with disabilities in a different light.

I do know for me, and I'm sure a lot of young women within this age bracket, that I have to be very mindful of what I consume on social media. In my opinion, social media is not all reality. Even though that's a very simple thing to say, it's a lesson that took me a long time to learn because we're looking on social media, and we're scrolling past the posts showing that everybody's having an amazing time. They're going on holidays, they're fit, they're healthy, eating well, and like we're only human, at the end of the day, we are going to let that get to us at some point. Especially if we are not in a strong frame of mind. Are we going to be on top notch, or not every day? Are we going to be strong willed human beings? We're going to have our slippery slopes days, and that's where I need to be very mindful. I need to make sure on those types of days that I don't let the 'perfect image' of what's being portrayed get me down.

Teenagers online worry me as they can be quite vulnerable and we all know that trolling is rampant out there. I just think it's really important to be mindful of what you share and also what you comment on people's posts. A kind word is so much better than a cruel one and the lasting effects of both on our mental health are very real.

I do think sometimes that I used social media as a comfort blanket and although I am not a control freak, I do have some controlling tendencies. I was able to connect with people in the way that suited me and have them get to know my personality rather than my shell. When it came time to tell people about my disability, I would often panic. I'm still a 'work in progress' and don't want to be defined by my disability or chronic pain, so I still don't say everything that I feel and think. As my confidence grows over the years, that's improving though. When I meet people in person that I have connected with, they are often a bit shocked and sometimes feel they have to look after me. I suppose seeing me in person can be a bit of a shock and that's why I like to spend time getting to know them first. That way, they know me, for me. The majority of people are always kind to me but sometimes I can see from their body language that they are a bit taken aback.

That's ok though, I probably would be too if it were me. I am as authentic on social media as I can be right now. I'm not saying I wear a mask or hide who I truly am, but I don't show every single thing about myself all the time. I'm not playing a character or pretending to be someone I'm not. But like everyone else, there are some days when I just don't feel great and I have to slap on a smile anyway. We can be walking down the street smiling at people and they smile back, but who knows what's going on behind our smiles? I'm not superhuman and I have my ups and downs like everyone else.

We're all entitled to a private life in any way, shape, or form. And we share the parts of us that we want to share. We share the parts of us that are maybe going to resonate with other people and what's going in their lives that. I try not to do it in the victim kind of sense. And I try not to do it in a poor me sense. Even though on the average Tuesday, I probably would be in victim mode myself, I try not put that energy out into the universe because I know myself that that energy won't serve me well. And that's not going to resonate with people or help and support people who are going on going through the same thing I'm going through. I think I am quite passionate with telling my story and telling what I go through in life. It isn't a case of posting for the purpose of attention, it is to help and support people going through kidney failure, living with a condition like mine, because it is tough and it is difficult.

I will always use my platform as a space to try and help others. That help may be in the form of supporting someone who is in similar circumstances to me, or it may be in educating people about disabilities.

I simply want to raise more awareness around disabilities and mental health. I want to level out the playing field a little so that people can see that someone with a disability is just the same as them inside. Yes, I can also use it as a place to improve my life, by meeting new contacts and setting up a small business, but my main focus is on raising awareness and promoting equality and acceptance. I know I'm not perfect and I don't pretend to be. I'll always strive to be as real as I can be at that time and in doing so, I hope that it will touch the people it needs to touch and that they can feel heard, understood and valued. Social media has many pitfalls, but it also has many advantages. If I can use it to help and support people, then I will continue to do so for as long as possible.

CHAPTER 6

IDENTITY, SEXUALITY, SEX AND ME

This is a mercifully short chapter given its title! Here's what I've noticed. Most of the content created on social media tends to deal with the big three; issues surrounding 1) identity, 2) sex and 3) relationships. In this chapter, I am going to explore these issues in some detail. I will also discuss ways that social media can be used, in a positive way, to increase awareness of these issues.

Identity is a fundamental aspect of a person's life. It helps them to develop a sense of who they are and how they relate to the world around them. Having a healthy sense of identity is important for both children and adults and plays a huge role in their emotional development, as well as the development of their social relationships. For this reason, it's important to ensure that individuals with disabilities are able to develop and maintain healthy identities from a young age, especially as we are living in an era of instant swiping on our smartphones. All you have to do is to go to your local Shopping Centre, sit on a bench, and watch kids and teens passing, all like zombies with their heads down, gazing at their mobile phones!

This can be done through early intervention programmes designed to meet the emerging needs of young children with disabilities. Such programmes could aim to specifically identify the challenges that these children may face later in life, and help them to overcome these challenges so that they can lead fulfilling lives as adults.

Now, while these programmes are, at least to an extent, effective in helping children develop positive identities, they often don't address the needs of adults with disabilities – and here I am with this kinda unwelcome status. This is something that needs to change if we're going to make genuine steps to reduce the stigma and negative stereotypes that surround disability not just in Irish society but in all societies.

Hmm, on to those thorny issues of sexuality and sex which are, at the best of times, difficult to talk about but especially so in this time of 'cancel culture' and 'wokeness.' As with all material in this book, it's not my intention to offend anyone, but at the same time, I wish to speak my own truth and contribute meaningfully to this crucial area of expression as so many people feel fearful to get involved despite the fact these issues affect all of us.

In order to increase visibility of the issues around sex and sexuality faced by women with disabilities in society, I feel it is crucial that more media sources and organisations focus on representing a diverse range of female experiences in relation to disability both in a general and specific context. One way to achieve this is through greater representation of women with disabilities on and across social media. This is especially important as the Internet is a key resource for information for many kinds of people who may not have widespread or easy access to other media outlets or educational material. By giving diverse perspectives on sex and sexuality a platform online, we can begin to challenge various attitudes and misconceptions surrounding disability and sex.

With one in four people in the UK and 13% of the population in Ireland (almost 600,000 people) having some form of impairment or illness, this is an important issue that needs to be addressed if we are to work towards more inclusive societies in the future.

I always wondered what it would be like to lose my virginity. I think I had it built up in my mind as a magical fairy-tale scenario, one that would see me romanced and loved and full of the joys of making that transition. Isn't that the way almost every girl imagines it? Why shouldn't I want the same thing? Even though sex education wasn't especially forthcoming for me, or for many people with a disability, I still wanted to know about it. I wanted to know how it worked and what is supposed to happen. I often wondered how it would feel, who it would be with and how I would be afterwards. I'd heard others say they felt different and changed somehow once they took that step, but I thought that would be an even bigger one for me in my position.

I had such a mix of emotions around the subject, it's not as easy for a disabled person to approach sex as it is for others. There's a lot more for me to consider and worry about and that often felt unfair to me. I wanted to be able to enjoy that part of life in the same way as everyone else, but honestly, I was entering one of the hardest and most challenging periods of my life.

I lost my virginity at a very distressing time in my life. I was 19 and I had just been diagnosed with kidney failure. I didn't even think of the emotional side of having sex or anything of the sort. I just thought I didn't want to be stuck being a virgin anymore.

I probably didn't have the greatest experience. I wasn't traumatised or anything, but I didn't really understand what all the fuss was about, I knew I'd rushed things because of the emotional impact of my kidney diagnoses. So, at such a young age my life had just crashed down in front of my eyes when it should have been taking off instead. It didn't happen again for me for another 10 years, zilch for 10 years. I made a vow with myself that the next person I got involved with, I would really be in love with. I stuck to it, the next person I was with 10 years after the first, I really did love. I spent time learning what was right for me and I gained maturity before I opened up to being physical with someone again.

That made a big difference to how I experienced the whole thing, having the emotion there and feeling loved and supported made the actual act of sex something beautiful and nurturing for me. It felt like that was how it was supposed to be. I'd waited 10 years but it was worth it. I wish my experiences of sex were all like that, but they weren't.

There's been times in my life when I used sex as a coping mechanism, working out of my trauma. Sometimes in relationships we project our own issues onto the other, or simply subconsciously try to heal our pain through them. On the other hand, I think we gain a lot of self-awareness through our relationships with others, they are often our greatest teachers, especially if we have our hearts broken.

I used to think that if someone has sex with you then it must mean that they care about you on a deeper level too. I've come to see that's not always the case. Instead of using it to cover up my feelings I just had to surrender to whatever was going on with me. It not an easy thing to do, to just let go and surrender. Once you do it though, it's really freeing. It's like lots of difficult things that have happened to me, it can take me a while to accept it but when I do, I can see the good things that it brings to me and not focus on the things I think are being taken away from me. I've come to look at a lot of things that way, especially around my kidney diagnosis, I am always trying to find the positives.

CHAPTER 7

MY KIDNEYS AND ME

This picture represents the kidneys and me chapter. Throughout this chapter, I talk a lot, a lot about being vulnerable, grieving, and also surrendering to the process. And that's exactly what this photo represents. Even though I have struggled very much so with the grieving process of my kidneys, I have come to a space of acceptance. And this photo is very simplistic. I'm sitting in silence. I am sitting with myself, working through the grieving process, and moving to the acceptance, and accepting what is in my hands and reaching out. Reaching out to whatever life has to show me next. Reaching out to represent acceptance that I'm okay sitting in silence. It's a powerful message, it represents the work that I have done throughout the years, the challenges that I have had to face accepting them for what they are and moving forward and moving forward into a space of clarity.

A space of peace in a space of acceptance. Being okay with my grief, acknowledging my grief, and welcoming what is to come next, welcoming the next chapter in my life. That's what the hands represent. Reaching out and welcoming the next stage. And working through each stage as I meet it, being kind to myself, showing a sense of compassion.

Meeting myself where I'm at, at any given moment, helping myself to move forward and to not sit in the grief or in the resentment, or even in the anger, helping myself to move forward into a space that's more resourceful for me. I want this photo to represent that to each and every person that reads this chapter. It's okay to be sad. It's okay to have to experience grief. It's okay to feel however you feel but try not unpack there. This chapter represents resourcing yourself, so you can move forward into that space of acceptance into that space of self-kindness into that space of self-compassion.

Chronic Kidney Disease (CKD) is a general term used to describe any disease or disorder that affects your kidneys and causes them to function abnormally. There are many different causes for CKD, including diabetes, high blood pressure and a family history of kidney disease. As the disease progresses, the kidneys become less effective and eventually stop working altogether. When this happens, you will usually require kidney dialysis in order to compensate for the loss of kidney function. Many people who have CKD are unaware that they have the condition until they experience symptoms like fatigue, loss of appetite or weight loss. Having regular blood tests to check how well your kidneys are working can help you to keep track of your condition and identify any changes that may have occurred over time.

When it comes to my kidneys, I know I'm on borrowed time, I never even thought I'd make it to 18, then 21 then 30. Here I am, 36 years old. Even I'm shocked at that! It makes me anxious, as sometimes I wonder if today is going to be the day I lose the battle. I'm proud of how far I've come and I know it's mostly down to my survival instincts and willpower. If you put me in the middle of the woods, I'd survive, it just kicks in. I've defied all the odds and I'm proud of that. There's a lot wrong with me, but there's a lot right with me too. I just don't feel I'm ready to give up yet. I don't know if my body agrees with me though. I always fought against going on dialysis, it was the one thing I dreaded. It felt like the end for me.

Even the word, dialysis, is a massive trigger for me. Anytime my doctor ever mentioned the word dialysis, I shut him up straightaway. I simply wouldn't let him discuss it with me. It was never an option for me to have dialysis at home when I was diagnosed at 19. It is now though. I was terrified to discuss it or even believe it was real. When I see dialysis, I just see machines, I see tubes. I see lying on bed and I see sick all the time. I've spent my childhood in hospital hooked up to machines trying to stay alive and I don't want to go back to that.

I already have a breathing machine for night times and a mobility scooter and now I have to accept that I probably need dialysis. When I first thought of having a mobility scooter, I was really against it. I just thought it was for old ladies and people in worse off positions than me. It took me a while but I came round to idea when my brother bought me one. It took me a while to accept it and to see all the ways it could actually improve my life. I don't know if it's going to be the same for the dialysis. I'm scared I'll be bed-bound and sick all the time and that I'll have no quality of life at all.

Some days it's all just too much, I didn't have any of this as a teenager, but as my health has deteriorated, I need more and more interventions to stay alive. Sometimes I get to a point of wondering what the point in it all is and if it's even worth it and thinking like that just isn't me. I'm not a pessimist, I've always been an optimist so for me to reach that point is pretty big. I just keep seeing my freedom and my health being taken away piece by piece and I sometimes wonder what else I'm going to have to do to just get by.

I don't feel like somebody who's got kidney failure. I can totally relate to people who have a terminal illness when they do get that prognosis. They are sitting there and the doctor is telling them that they're on the way out and they can't believe it. They feel like there's nothing wrong with them. That's the thing about renal failure, it is the most silent thing on the planet and it's the most violent thing on the planet. It is something that needs to be watched, especially in people with spinal bifida, having kidney failure and having kidney problems is very, very common. I've fought this all the way and kept going but things are changing and it's not easy to admit that.

There's huge denial that comes into play too. When I was first diagnosed, I remember thinking the doctor must be wrong and telling him he needed to go back to college. I just didn't feel like someone with kidney failure. There's a mourning that happens with that. It's as if I'm mourning a piece of me that's dying. I can't just be told to get on with it, there's a process for me to go through in order to accept it. I think a lot more empathy is needed for people who get a prognosis like mine, we are mourning a part of ourselves, whether that be our kidneys or a woman having a hysterectomy or a cancer patient losing a part of their body. It's all about the loss and grief and acceptance. It's a process and it can't be rushed. I hope to see more help on offer to people in this position, more counselling and support. We can't just be told 'well that's the way it is, so you better get on with it'. We need time, understanding and a chance to go through the stages of grief as we say goodbye to the people we were before the diagnoses. We will be saying goodbye not only to parts of ourselves physically, but also activities we would have done before, friendships that we could uphold and aspirations we had that may be affected by it.

I feel like I've been living on a tightrope for the last 16 years and that any minute I'm going to fall off it. In general though I try not to focus too much on the fear part of it, I go to talk therapy and that helps me so much. It stops me sweeping stuff under the carpet. I like to try to remember that my health is just a part of me, it isn't my soul. Yes, my health is like a roller coaster, but it's not all there is to me. I still love to have the banter and the craic too. I've learned to calm the fight or flight mode by remembering how I can help people to take their own power back over their lives regardless of their circumstances, so even though my mind works at 99% capacity at all times, I try and focus on all the good things I still have and all the things I can offer to help others.

At present I'm working on 10% kidney function, I have been for the last 16 years. I'm like the cat with 9 lives, it's unheard of. I'm in the middle of very serious juggling act at the moment, I've a 90% blockage in my neck. It is possible to unblock it, and if it was anyone else without my ailments that would have been done already. Stenting is just a temporary solution, it normally only lasts between 2 to 5 years. The problem with doing that now is that you have to put a dye in so the surgeon can see the blockage. The scary part is that dye could really damage my kidneys, therefore it's extremely dangerous for me in my current situation. That bit of dye could really wipe my kidneys out and put me on dialysis for the rest of my life, or until I'd be a candidate for a kidney transplant. I'm not even sure I'd be suitable for that.

So I have decided to leave the blockage in my neck even though it is quite sore at times. Also, it is quite painful at times. I can't overexert myself a hell of a lot because it will put pressure on it and then that's blockage drains the blood from the head, the face and the neck. So as you can imagine, my face is a little bit more swollen than it should be. And for somebody like myself that takes pride in my face because I have scoliosis, it's very important to me.

I will admit that it is a vanity thing. We all have elements of vanity within our character. I think it doesn't matter who we are, we all want to be pretty and nice and do whatever we can to make ourselves attractive. By attractive I mean whatever is acceptable for us. I do have a disfigurement that's quite noticeable, so having an attractive face is kind of essential to me. So yes, at present I've decided to leave the blockage because the risk is just too high for me. I can't speak for anybody else, but for me, the risk is just far too high.

I am working on the acceptance piece when it comes to dialysis. But it is a massive struggle for me. It's not one of those things that has come easily to me, like a lot of things in life, I've had to struggle. And I've accepted an awful lot in life. It's just really hard for me to accept that my kidneys are failing, because I guess I have worked so hard over the last 16 years to keep them above water.

To be honest, it's probably been one of the hardest predicaments that I've had to date. I know I've had major surgeries in the past, but they've been surgeries that I've needed to do. They've been life and death, I didn't really have a choice.

This is the first time that I've felt like an adult, because when it comes to the blockage in my head, I've had to make my own decisions. I kept asking mum and Dr Casserly to tell me what to do, I just didn't know what to do. It was really hard for mum to see me reach out for help like that and for her to tell me that this one was my choice. She's been with me through this since the beginning so she knows how vulnerable I feel. This is the first time I've felt a bit more out on my own, having to make my own mind up. I'm at a crossroads and whatever path I choose I feel like I can't really win. I can only keep afloat for as long as possible. It's really not a place I'm comfortable with just yet. I feel like there is no right or wrong here, there are risks either way. So rather than leave it up to the universe, I decided not to do the surgery and to see how I cope.

Albert Einstein once said: "I must be willing to give up what I am in order to become what I will be."

I have been grappling with the decision of whether or not to undergo Kidney Dialysis. After much thought and consideration, I have decided that undergoing the treatment is something that I am finally willing to consider. Having experienced various levels of kidney function over the past few years, I feel that I have a pretty good understanding of what the side effects of dialysis will be like as well as what symptoms to look out for. However, there are still a number of concerns that I have had around the treatment that I would like to address before moving forward. Below are some of the things that have been weighing heavily on my mind in recent months.

As I mentioned, I have lived with chronic kidney disease for the past 16 years. During this time, I have experienced an array of symptoms ranging from kidney stones to excessive fatigue. Over the years, these have waxed and waned as my kidney function has fluctuated from month to month. Currently, I am experiencing symptoms of much more severe kidney damage. Fortunately, I am still able to work and financially support myself so the decision to undergo dialysis has, in some senses been both a huge struggle and a decision that I had to make. But, more about that shortly.

Recently, I have started to experience much more persistent pain around my lower back and abdomen to name but two areas. There are more but I'll spare the details! I have also noticed an increase in the frequency of my trips to the bathroom, especially at night and overall, I am feeling very fatigued a lot of the time and my energy levels are very low compared to how they were just a few years ago. At this point, I am not sure what the future holds for me and, of course, I know this is true of anyone but it has brought my life into a clearer lens. Essentially, I feel like the time has come to make THE decision about (a) whether or not I will undergo dialysis (b) where this will take place and (c) what format it will take. Here are a few of the things that I have been thinking about and anyone facing a similar issue will probably think of this too:

**1. What to expect from my treatment with Kidney Dialysis.

Kidney Dialysis is the process of cleansing the blood of toxins and maintaining the balance of fluids and salts in the body. It involves the removal of blood from the veins of the body and circulating it through a filter that removes waste and excess fluid before returning it to the bloodstream. During the treatment, the patient is connected to a machine via a catheter inserted into the vein in his arm or leg. Blood is drawn from one arm into the machine where it is filtered and then returned back to the body through the other arm.

Typically, the procedure lasts about four hours but may vary according to the needs of each individual patient. The patient will be hooked up to the machine for the duration of this time and is expected to remain as comfortable as possible throughout the procedure. After the treatment is completed, the patient can return home to rest. The effects of the treatment will depend on the severity of your condition and whether or not it was successful at clearing your kidneys of excess fluids and waste. In most cases, patients will need to continue receiving regular treatments until they are feeling well again and their kidney function has improved. In some cases, however, it is possible that you will require on-going treatment for the rest of your life.

**2. Are there any alternative treatment options that I could try before undergoing Kidney Dialysis?

There are a variety of alternative treatment options that could assist in the management of your condition before resorting to Kidney Dialysis. These include: antibiotics, blood transfusions, kidney support supplements and blood pressure medications. While some of these options may not be suitable for an individual's particular condition, it is important to discuss them with your doctors and medical team in order to determine the most appropriate course of action for you. I am finding this is really an individual thing.

**3. What can I do to ensure that my Kidney Dialysis treatment is as comfortable as possible?

This might appear to be a strange one but, a comfortable dialysis environment is important to the treatment process and to your overall wellbeing during recovery. This is because treatment sessions generally last anywhere between three and five hours and it is therefore important to ensure that you are as comfortable and relaxed as possible during this time.

I will have to get my house renovated to accommodate treatment at home. So, the questions I have had to ask myself are, is setting up home dialysis an option for me? If so, how would I prepare my home for dialysis treatment? What are the likely costs? How much disruption will this bring to my life and my family?

**4. How long will I need to receive Kidney Dialysis treatment for?

A fourth huge issue will obviously depend on a number of factors, including the type of treatment you are having and the number of treatments you might need each week. Once you have finished your first session, you should meet with your doctor to discuss your progress and decide whether you will need to continue having further treatments.

You may also be advised to undergo additional tests in order to monitor your progress and assess the health of your kidneys. You should also speak to your doctor about the possibility of taking part in a clinical trial in the future, as this may help to improve your treatment outcomes.

As I move now towards the end of writing my book, I've come to the decision that it will soon be time for me to begin the dialysis. I never thought I would reach this point and I put it off for as long as possible. I simply didn't want to admit that it was necessary and didn't want my freedom, as I saw it, to be taken away from me. It's a huge commitment to make as it takes hours a day to see it through. Hospital dialysis in four hours per session, 3 days a week. To do it at home, it's four days a week.

So, as you can see, it's not something to be taken on lightly.

I have reached the point, however, where I really don't see any other option. If I don't do it, I will deteriorate past the point of having any quality of life. I can't put this off any longer or I will lose this battle. I think I've done pretty well to put it off this long and still live the full life I have. The tides are turning though and I know if I want to carry on, I have to do this. You will understand why this has taken me a long time to accept and hopefully you will also understand that it won't be easy for me. I don't expect to be jumping for joy when it starts and I will have to mind my mental health too while going through this. I will need to make sure I'm doing everything I can to stay positive and upbeat. I know I'll need a space to talk about my worries and fears around this and to share how I find it impacts me physically. I'll be sitting in the one spot for a few hours a day, unable to suddenly decide I've had enough and go and do something different.

The acceptance that I need to do it is only the first stage in this. Then comes the other stuff, the practicalities of putting it all in place and beginning it. Then, getting used to the different routine in my life every day and all the emotions that come with that. I expect to feel grief and perhaps some anger and frustration. As long as I can process all the feelings, I think I'll be ok. It won't be easy but like I said, I still have a lot to give in this life and if dialysis will allow me to carry on then I'll do it and face it head on as best I can.

I know I'll be depending on family a bit more at this time in lots of different ways. I'm sure I will need their help with all the practical parts but also, I'll need my mum close by to talk to. She's always been such a good listener when it comes to me and I don't imagine it being any different then. It's a bitter sweet pill I have to swallow, I'm sacrificing something for the sake of something greater, but in my opinion, it's worth it. I came to the decision largely due to the fact that I have a niece who I want to be able to see grow up and the love I feel for her fuelled my final decision. She is a hugely important part of my life and if the dialysis will help me be around for her for more time, then I'll gladly do it.

CHAPTER 8

THE WHITE HAIR TRIBE

Irish family crests, also known as coats of arms, represent your Irish heritage in colors and symbols. Each of these stands for something significant about your family background. What stands out of me the most in my family's Crest in the 3 Lions, I being a Leo myself!

Sometimes we have to look past the hard shell and see the person as a whole and valuable human being who may be acting out feelings of fear, frustration, anger, hurt or insecurity. Understand that there may be valid reasons for those feelings and try to exercise empathy. Being lion-like means you are brave and courageous; Bravery to find what really makes me happy; Bravery to ignore what others feel is successful and find my own success; Bravery to dare to make changes in my path.

A person with a lion mindset is determined to achieve their goals in life. There is more focusing on doing the tough work and seeing the results rather than just dreaming about getting somewhere. Some people are naturally born with a lion mindset or they are nurtured in a way that they adopt that Mindset. I have no doubt in my mind that my family have nurtured me and helped me adopt this mindset.

In this chapter I would like to talk about being a Mungovan. I spoke about my family in my first book quite a bit but there's always more to share and maybe a little more on the name 'Mungovan'.

Throughout my whole life Mungovan has been mispronounced and, by God, have we seen it being spelt all kinds of ways. I remember there was one time I was visiting my brother who lives in England with his wife and now my beautiful niece. I was waiting in the airport in the assistance area to board my flight home. When I travel now, I opt for assistance. I have grown to realise that its ok to ask for help every now and then. Over the intercom I hear a name being called out, 'Sio Ban Mongavin'. This name was repeated a few times and I found myself getting annoyed, wishing they would answer the poor man so I can get on board myself and, let's face it, I was getting impatient. A few seconds later, it dawned on me that it was me they were calling! I was mortified!

In recent years, I have become more and more interested in my family name, its meaning and background. Throughout my research I was surprised to find they wasn't much information available but I was delighted to find some interesting bits all the same.

As for the name Mungovan, you may not know the Gaelic version of the name is O'Mongobhain....from the Gaelic "Mong" or sometimes "Muing"..."mane" and even "bán"...white. Essentially, Mungovan means in its direct English translation "white maned" or "Whitehead." They took the name from their hair colour. Mungovan is a very rare family name, few people in United States and Ireland have the last name. Only around 579 people have been found who have Mungovan as their family name.

There were 114 with this surname in Ireland way back in 1901. The surname was ranked 3631st in Ireland in the same year, MURPHY was ranked 1st since it is the most common Irish surname.

How likely are you to meet someone with the last name of Mungovan? Chances are, most people haven't met someone with Mungovan as their last name since less than 1 person in 909k people have that last name. If you know one, consider yourself lucky!

Here is a little family tree to give you some understanding as to how little old Siobhán entered this world.

James Mungovan and Mary Ann Reidy Mungovan gave birth to my grandfather John Joe, or Sean, known to his sisters (of which he had eleven) on the 4th July 1917. Even though John Joe passed away in Aug 1988 and I was only two years of age I have been told down through the years I have the same spirit as him. John Joe Mungovan married Nora Queally and, in turn, had nine children, four girls and five boys, one of which was my dad, Noel Mungovan. Noel met and married a beautiful west Clare lady by the name of

Geraldine O Halloran, my mam in 1984. I am sure he knew he hit the jackpot when he married my mam on that day.

Noel and Geraldine had three children; Shane, Siobhán and Conor. I was born into the world on Wednesday the 30th July 1986 and given the name Siobhán. Siobhán is another form of the name 'Joan', and means 'God has been gracious' or 'God's grace'. It can also mean 'full of charm'. I am sure a few of you reading this would agree with the charm but I am not sure if that's a good or bad thing!

My Family have been my rock throughout my life, each of them in different ways. Each member of my family has brought something unique into my journey and I'm grateful to them for all of it.

Okay, so I guess my family network is just like every other person's family network. Throughout our years growing up, I guess we have been quite a 'serious' family. We have our ups and downs just like every other family. There have been times when we have laughed and joked and done silly things just like everybody else.

I don't really speak too much about my relationship with my dad. When I was in hospital during Covid-19 times, my relationship with dad improved because I could see a lot more of what he did for me. I talked about him in a previous chapter but I felt I could understand him in a way I hadn't before. He might not always have been able to talk to me about the serious stuff, but he brought laughter into my life. That, in and of itself, is a type of medicine. It provides a sort of balance in comparison to my relationship with mum, but I'll talk more about mum shortly.

A lot of my time that I spent with my dad was in the car, because I don't drive. And that's a blessing to everybody on the road, not just me. I simply wasn't very good at it. So my dad drives me to and from work. But there was one day I was come coming home from work, we were chatting away in the car and he was asking me how my day was and I asking him how his day was. And this is back in the time when my dad smoked.

He told me he needs to stop for some cigarettes but I noticed there were five sitting in the front seat that belonged to my brother Shane (bearing in mind we were in a van with only two seats and nothing in the back). Dad said he couldn't smoke them as they were Shane's and I told him, 'go ahead, he's really annoyed me today!' I went on and on about how much Shane had pissed me off that day until I heard laughing from the back of the van! Would you believe it was Shane, sitting in the back of the van where I couldn't see him! Dad and Shane were both in wrinkles laughing, doubled over to the point of being in hysterics.

Needless to say, I was mortified; I've never been so embarrassed in my life. I'd been sitting slagging him off and all the time he could hear me. Thank goodness he has a sense of humour and didn't take offense.

My Dad is very old school but every so often, he loves to wind me up! One more example is when we were in the van again and he convinced me that there was an actual pony in the back, covered with a blanket because it was asleep. I went into shock; I couldn't believe it! I've always wanted a pony, I was there, heavy breathing with anticipation of seeing this thing! Of course, it didn't occur to me at the time that it wasn't making any noise, I was too excited to pay attention to that.

It took me ages to work out that he was joking and that it was a rocking horse!! He was in stitches, and this carried on until I got home. He did that kind of thing randomly, or whenever things were a bit tense between us, or if we had had words with each other, to break the ice a bit. I love that about him. It's his way of showing emotion. He does struggle with finding the words to express it, so he shows that he cares through his actions. He's very solid and dependable, and it's through the little things that he does every day that he shows he loves us.

Mum, on the other hand, is more vocal with her care and worry for me. She is always by my side at hospital appointments and communicates her concerns with me and lets me share mine with her. They balance each other out like that. I get the best of both worlds. I don't know what I would do without her, she's been my right-hand woman for all my life, fighting my corner with me. She might not always agree with me or my decisions, or me with hers, but we share a very strong bond that is a massive support for me.

I don't know what I'll do when either of my parents pass away. The very thought of it terrifies me. I've never experienced a loss of a close loved one and I've no idea how I will cope when they aren't here to be watching me and making sure I'm ok. When I even think about it, my whole body reacts physically. My heart beats faster, I feel like I can't breathe and that I might have a panic attack. My heart literally feels like it's going to explode with fear and dread.

The emotion around it all is debilitating for me, it sends me into a state of utter shock and terror. The pain that I know I will feel when the time comes, is something I'm not sure I will be able to handle at all. I've never felt anything like it, it's overwhelming for me. That might not sound very rational, we all know our parents will pass away one day, but the anticipation of that coming to me in the future is enough to break me. I write about this again later.

Moving on to other family members, Shane is a wonderful brother, in fact he has been like a second father figure to me throughout the years. That's the good thing about having a big brother, it's another strong man to lean on at times. I don't think I've always been the easiest little sister for him, but he doesn't seem to mind. He's always been protective over me, even when my rebellious side would show itself and I'd try to do the opposite of what he thought was right for me. He always tried, in a loving and kind way, to show me what I could and couldn't do, even if I didn't agree with him. He must have the patience of a saint with me. I would tend to try things and deal with the consequences after, whereas he tried to prevent bad things happening to me. He's very protective of me and would try to make sure no harm came to me.

Growing up, I had a bit of a 'queen bee' mentality with him, people around me used to call me that sometimes. I'd hand him my school bag and expect him to carry it for me. Sometimes, I pushed it a bit and I can see now, looking back, how some of my behaviours certainly fell into the 'queen bee' category. He never gave me a hard time about it though, I think he gave me a bit of a pass on that one. Sometimes I simply refused to do things that I was capable of, like getting something from the shed or bringing in some turf for the fire. I was called out on it a few times and I know that's because my family wanted me to be as independent as possible, so the 'queen bee' thing had to stop. I realised I couldn't pick and choose the things I wanted to do if I expected to be taken seriously. I'm glad I wasn't allowed to get away with too much, it did really help me when it was time for me to move out and into my own home. If I'd not been allowed to lift a finger at home with my family, there's no way I would have known how to run my own home. He lives in England now but we do try and talk all the time and he's able to come home often enough.

I have a younger brother too who I'd like to mention. We have a bit of a different dynamic going on. While my older brother is like a father figure to me, my younger one reminds me of what it's like to have fun. We have a lot of craic together and especially when he has friends around and everyone is laughing and showing each other things on the phone. For a moment, I forget I have these conditions. That's what he brings into my life, the sense of being young and carefree. I value that a lot.

I believe that each person in a family has a role to play and that each role is valuable. It's kind of like a play, we all interact with each other, and we all have our own lines to say and contribute to the overall story. I think that when you break it down, each person brings something different to the table. We all have our own individual health problems and sometimes the feeling within the family has been heavy and serious. I notice when we all get together that we can lighten that and bounce off each other. I haven't made it easy for them, especially not when I was a teenager and during my time of the month when I had my period. My hormones would have been all over the place and I was just coming to terms with my conditions, so I often made sure they knew just how much I was suffering and that it must be worse than their pain. That wasn't really fair on them and thankfully over the years, as I've matured, I don't need to do that anymore.

Becoming an auntie for the first time

Over the last year I became an aunt for the first time. For me, this the best feeling in the world. It's the best and a pure elation of happiness!! *BEST AND MOST IMPORTANT DAYS* of my 36 years life so far. Ava is the newest (and by far the cutest) member of my family. I know I am biased but I love this feeling.

After seeing hundreds of photos of Ava and viewing countless videos, suddenly the day came where I got to meet her for the very first time, and there she was, right in front of me! It was a surreal moment but also a very joyful one. She was even more precious and beautiful in person as she was through the various media I watched. I feel like the world was going in slow motion, nothing else mattered but living in the present moment in this love bubble.

My brother brought her over to me in his arms and I got my first up close view. My mam then held her for a second. They then asked if I was ready to hold her. I said 'yes'. I was terrified but our first moment together was full of smiles and peace. She was so tiny! Her hair was so soft! She made such cute little noises!

As soon as I met my niece, I felt so naturally comfortable around her. She was immediately part of the family, and I felt instantly connected to her. I guess this was something I was very nervous about and, as crazy as it sounds, my insecurities came to the surface thinking to myself to myself would she judge me for being different?

Completely irrational I know. I like to think that she's already made me a more selfless person.

I do feel she has changed our family dynamics as I mentioned earlier we are quite a serious family but I feel Ava has brought out the fun side to us all. There is something special watching someone who is only seeing and experiencing things for the first time. You know, the 'beginners eye'. In a day and age where emigration is very high here in Ireland I do consider myself lucky that she only lives close by in England. People say that having a child teaches you many lessons about life, love, and what it truly means to be human.

But even if you don't have one of your own, being an aunt can also teach you very many valuable things. You may ask what have I learned with being an aunt for the first time well I have learned more about myself than anything else.

She has taught me to slow down and enjoy the simple things in life again. Sometimes we can live our life in the fast lane trying to keeping up with everything around you. When I spend time with Ava one of my favourite things to do is sit on the floor with her and just play with her toys and watch her clap and giggle.

She has helped me to tap into the child like part of myself again which was weird for me because I had to grow up so fast. I feel she has brought the child out in all of us within the family To sum it up so far, what it's like to be a first time aunt is: amazing.

I can't wait to watch her grow into a beautiful strong lady. I hope, as an aunt, I can provide stability and an escape from day to day and be someone that she can turn to if needed.

CHAPTER 9

COVID-19

I've left this chapter until this point in my book because we are still living in the Covid-19 era. This chapter/photo represents COVID-19. It represents fear, protecting myself from the unknown Afraid of being out of control and not knowing what's going to happen. This photo also represents a lot of aspects of my life where I have felt out of control, where I have felt that I haven't been in control of my health, where there is a sense of sadness in the eyes, the sense of looking into one's soul, looking deep within to see what's really going on behind the shell, what was going on for me during this time, the COVID-19 period of my life. A time where I was locked away, a time where I had to protect myself from something that we could not see yet, staying connected. It also represents reconnecting with myself and getting comfortable in my own skin. And in this photo, you can see that I am hugging myself. So, I am introducing myself to myself for the first time.

Covid-19 is a respiratory condition caused by a virus which attacks the lungs, making it difficult to breathe, and can lead to serious complications such as pneumonia and other respiratory diseases. According to the World Health Organisation, about 15% of people who contract COVID-19 will develop pneumonia.

With these serious complications, it is critical that individuals take precautions and practice proper hygiene to prevent the spread of the virus. For instance, individuals should regularly wash their hands for 20 seconds, avoid touching their face, and practice social distancing when in public. Without prompt treatment, the virus can be fatal in some cases. For instance, the virus is particularly dangerous for elderly people, as well as those with pre-existing health conditions, such as diabetes, heart disease, and respiratory diseases. To what extents exactly are still being debated in research and the media!

However, there are also many people who contract the virus but experience only mild symptoms and recover quickly. In fact, we now know that most people who contract the virus will recover without any serious health complications. Recent research suggests that people without symptoms are less likely to transmit the virus than those who develop symptoms. For example, one study found that only 0-2.2% of people with asymptomatic infection infected anyone else, compared to 0.8-15.4% of people with symptoms.

Asymptomatic means having a disease or condition but not experiencing any symptoms of it. It's like a fire that has been smouldering in an area that may not have been checked in a while. The fire is still burning, but it hasn't reached a point where it's visible or causing any alarm until it starts to spread. Asymptomatic individuals have been found to be responsible for 40 to 45 percent of infections, according to a review of data from 16 contact-tracing studies.

Covid-19 has been particularly difficult for people with disabilities as many people with disabilities rely on support services, such as transportation and personal care attendants to help them get by on a daily basis. The pandemic has caused many of these services to be severely disrupted or cancelled, leaving people with disabilities with fewer resources to rely on.

This disruption has been especially challenging for those with disabilities, as it has left them with limited options to maintain their independence and quality of life. For example, a person with a disability relying on an attendant to help them get to the local food store may be unable to access the necessary food and supplies they need to live independently.

Women with disabilities that have or have had a history of cancer are often at a higher risk of developing complications from Covid-19, like pneumonia and blood clots in the lungs. However, not all women with health conditions will necessarily be at a higher risk for the complications of Covid-19. The ways in which a woman's disability affects her risk for infection is variable and depends on factors such as the severity of the disability and whether or not the woman has taken any medications that affect the immune system. A woman who is dependent on a ventilator for breathing, as an example, will be at an increased risk of developing complications from the disease because of her weakened immune system. On the other hand, a woman who has amyotrophic lateral sclerosis or another neurodegenerative disorder will not be at an increased risk of contracting Covid-19 because these conditions generally do not weaken the immune system.

In an article published by the National Institute of Health in April of 2020, it was reported that women who are on oestrogen replacement therapy are at a greater risk of developing severe symptoms if they contract the virus. This finding was based on the results of a small clinical trial in France involving seven women who were undergoing treatment for breast cancer when they contracted Covid-19. All of the women developed severe symptoms of Covid-19, including a fever, shortness of breath, and rapid weight loss. All seven of the women in the study were also receiving tamoxifen therapy for breast cancer. Tamoxifen is an oestrogen receptor antagonist that prevents the release of oestrogen in the body by blocking the action of enzymes called aromatase.

I think Covid-19 has a had lasting effect on me, both good and bad. Before Covid-19, I wouldn't have been great at being in my own company, I would have quite happily kept myself busy to avoid being alone. I often went out every night doing different activities, just so I didn't have to sit at home with my thoughts and feelings. It wasn't that I didn't like myself, I just had a lot of worries and anxieties that would come to the surface once I was alone. Getting out and doing stuff meant I didn't have to think too much and I could focus on connecting with people.

When Covid-19 hit however, I had no choice. None of us did. Everything was taken away from us. I never would have made the choice to stay in and get comfortable in my own skin unless I had been forced to. So, in a way, I'm thankful for it. I had to move my life out of the fast lane and into something entirely different. I had to slow down, I had to learn to be by myself and be ok with it. Covid-19 meant I had no choice but to get comfortable with being in my own company and all the anxieties that came up for me.

I have no doubt in my mind that I am suffering from Medical PTSD as I get older even though I have not been formally diagnosed and I am not one for putting labels on myself. I am one that's easily frightened. Just ask my mam! I am always on the look out of danger and need to be prepared for all events home dialysis is just one example. If I sat at home and had a headache, as far as I was concerned, my head would have been falling off and I would have catastrophised everything. When I was out and about I was able to distract myself from that.

I suppose I had been pushing myself to live a full life and avoid bad news or diagnoses because I felt I had something to prove to my parents, as if I was showing them that I'm still active, I'm still here. If I was busy all the time, then I could avoid thinking about kidney dialysis or anything else medical for that matter. I was able to feel as normal as I possibly could. Having to stop and go into lockdown changed that, all the things I had been avoiding thinking about were right there waiting for me to pay them attention. In some ways, being very socially active kept me strong and kept me going. It was a big shock to my system when I couldn't be that way for a long time.

Covid-19 made me accept my limitations. That word, limitations, wasn't even in my vocabulary before the national lockdowns came in. It was really hard for me to lose contact with people but at least for once, I felt like I wasn't the odd one out. We were all in the same boat, we were all equal. Everybody's loneliness was hitting them as there was such a lack of social activity and connection. I just felt at least I wasn't the only one going through it and it was reassuring for me. It was probably the first time I felt just like everyone else, there was something comforting in that.

The bad side of Covid-19 for me was that I ended up in hospital for seven weeks during the height of it. I was quite sick and not being able to have family come to visit me was terrible. Anytime I had been in hospital before, I'd had visitors and support. I couldn't have visits this time. Covid-19 took away that comfort, it took away the reassurance of my Mum being able to be by my side when I wasn't well. There were people who died alone, with nobody there to hold their hands. That really affected me, I felt really scared and alone and I found it really hard to communicate my needs. Mum would normally have been my voice with the doctors at times when I was ill and couldn't speak up for myself, which wasn't often as I can say what I need to them, but having to do it all alone felt like an extra cruel hand had been dealt to me when I was at a low point. The hospital simply couldn't give me what I needed, it wasn't allowed and I felt trapped. I felt like I was behind bars, screaming to be heard but nobody would listen to me. I felt deeply sad and as if I had no way out.

It was a time when I felt so alone and scared, more than ever before in any hospital situation. I know the medical staff were doing their best, but it was terrifying for me. I even rang my Mum a few times and told her she needed to come and pick me up because I panicked, I felt like I was in jail. I couldn't breathe properly, I felt so afraid, and I just wanted out of there. My body would shake with the fear and all I could think about was how I could orchestrate a way out. I was used to having my person there, my nominated next of kin, for every twist and turn. It was the first taste of what it will be like when I no longer have my parents and I really didn't like it. That was a big negative of Covid-19 for me, having to go through that on my own, lying in hospital with nobody able to sit with me and help me.

I guess you could say I feel resentful towards Covid-19 for taking away my comfort in those times. I feared for my life when I was in hospital in Cork and thought I might die alone.

That time definitely gave me a much deeper appreciation for my parents and everyone else in my support network. I've always had gratitude for them, but it's on a whole new level now.

I have noticed my health has deteriorated a bit since Covid-19 times. My lungs aren't great. I think maybe that's to do with not getting out as much and exercising them. My legs still get me around the house though, or a walk around work. I want to keep using them for as long as I'm blessed with them functioning! I've tried to get back to normal life as much as possible, I'm still out and about and seeing people but I'm more aware of my limitations now and more accepting of what is good and bad for me.

I used to have a huge fear of missing out but that's not as bad these days, I feel more in control of that. I feel more comfortable saying no to things now. In particular I feel more comfortable with who I am, I know I'm not everyone's cup of tea but I know I'm alright, I'm a good person.

Covid-19 really impacted my relationships with my family too. I was so used to being able to see my Mum whenever we wanted to, that having to isolate from her was extremely difficult and painful, for both of us. I felt really disconnected from everyone then. I found that really lonely at times and felt scared without her around at times, although eventually I believe it did make me stronger and more independent.

One stand-out moment for me was when we were able to meet, at a distance, on Mother's Day in a carpark. Like most other people, I loved spending time with my Mum on Mother's Day. We didn't always go out somewhere but we would have always made sure to have lunch together or just see each other so I could give her a card and a hug. I was determined to try and find a loophole where I could still see her, but in a safe way for us both.

As funny as it might sound, we decided to meet in a carpark and have a takeaway meal but to sit at a good distance from each other. We are both vulnerable in our own ways so we had to make sure to keep the other person safe from any chance of infection. So, we sat at two ends of the carpark as if we were at the kitchen dining table. it's madness thinking about it now but it was the only option we had at the time. My relationship with her is, and always has been, of utmost importance to me, so I didn't want to let her down on Mother's Day.

It might have looked funny from the outside but my brother was running in between us at times, telling one of us what the other one was saying if we couldn't hear it! Bless him, he really tried to make it a nice day for us too. We were shouting requests across the car park at each other and discussing future plans when Covid-19 calmed down and I think it gave us both something to look forward to. It gave us some hope for the future. It was a day I really needed to spend with her and although we didn't get long, it was enough to give me the strength to keep going and to look forwards. I came away from there feeling more connected and less alone.

That's the thing with humans, we are meant for connection and belonging. We aren't designed to be alone all the time, we are meant to be part of families and communities, it's where we thrive. So on that note, I think Covid-19 and lockdowns really made a lot of people feel isolated and disconnected. While it's imperative to keep each other safe, it's also important to find ways to still connect, even if it's by video call. Mum isn't that knowledgeable about social media and video calls, but she's learning, a lot of people had to learn in those days just to keep in touch with the outside world.

I missed not being able to hold her hand. Her hand was the first one I ever held in my life. I'm an affectionate person and quite 'huggy', so I really missed that aspect of things. The physical distance was hard. Even now, when I look at her hand, I see my grandmothers. That's just the ageing process I know, but there's comfort in it for me. The generations of women who have been there in my family are there in those hands.

It's not just the relationship with my mum that was impacted either through Covid-19. An unexpected twist was that being in hospital really brought my Dad and I together. I love the man to bits and have always had a good relationship with him, but I found myself drawing even closer to him, asking after him, worrying about him.

Things with Mum have always been amazing and I know it's natural to navigate towards one parent, but the thought of him not being around put things into perspective. Something deeper hit me in hospital, a better understanding of what he does and how much he means to me. That's been a really good thing about Covid-19, I'm grateful for him more than ever now. I can see more of who he is as a man and as father. I didn't expect that so it was a bit of a shock. I'm glad for it though, that whole time has improved my understanding of both my parents and their importance in my life. I believe that Covid-19 did that for a lot of people, I hear people say how they realised all the things they had taken for granted up until that point. Family relationships being one of them.

Health being another. The ability to take part in social activities is also something that was swiftly removed during Covid-19. Meeting up and being a part of group activities isn't something any of us thought would become obsolete for a period of time.

Take this for example. I'm a member of the Ennis Musical Society and I love it. They are like family to me. Just before Covid-19 hit, we were working together on a production of something similar to 'Cat In The Hat' and had been rehearsing together for 3 or 4 months. Everyone knows you live in each other's pockets during rehearsals, you are family during that time. We had done two shows then we got the news that Covid-19 was hitting. It had been talked about but no lockdowns or actions had been put in place until then. We got word that a lockdown was coming in and we were utterly heartbroken. We had put months of sweat and tears into this production and now we were going to have to cancel our show. It was devastating.

The pubs were still open and everyone was still allowed out at that stage, so we all went out of a drink before the first lockdown was due to happen at midnight the next day. I didn't get home until 7am the next morning, we gave the show and each other a great send off because we knew we wouldn't be seeing each other for a long time to come. It was one of the best nights I've ever had. That's the thing, we didn't expect it (the lockdown) to be as long as it was, 6 or 8 months. We didn't know how meeting socially would become an alien thing, let alone an illegal thing, for so long.

One important thing to mention is that nobody expected when the lockdowns began to lift, that a lot of us would still be very cautious about meeting. In the beginning, we all talked about how great it would be to get back to normal and how excited we were to meet again. However, I found once restrictions began to lift, I wasn't as keen as I had been. Just because it was now legal, didn't mean it felt safe. I think a prolonged period of time in isolation and in fear meant that a lot of people were still carrying that feeling when it was permitted to meet and go out again. I've noticed how the number of people returning back to social events just isn't the same as it was pre-covid-19. Some people are still scared and still isolate as much as possible.

I understand that, being classed as vulnerable myself, I want to protect myself and others. On the other hand, I do think it's important to return slowly and safely into the world again. Social interaction and belonging are essential to mental health and all round wellbeing.

I did contract Covid-19 myself and with 10% lung capacity, it was a huge fear for the people around me that it would be the death of me. I suppose I sort of dismissed their worries. I was lucky I had no more than a dry throat. I felt generally fine, but I kept waking up every day thinking that would be the day that it hit me hard. I did get very anxious about that as the 10 days went on but thankfully, it really wasn't too bad for me. I didn't even tell my doctor until it was nearly over. He said I was probably so used to being sick that I barely noticed it!

I know people are getting it more than once so if it happens again to me, I'm stubborn enough to believe I'll get through it. That's always been my mindset.

I found online therapy really helpful for me during Covid-19 and the lockdowns, I never could have given that up. Having a third party to help me through this time was invaluable. It was important that it was someone with no emotional attachment to what I was saying. My emotions were all a bit elevated throughout it all, so having that hour to talk to someone made all the difference to me.

One thing that came up a lot for me was that I'm 36 and I haven't lost anyone I dearly love yet. One of my biggest fears in life has been grief yet I've never experienced it. It made me feel out of control because the threat of losing people seemed more real with Covid-19. There was something about the reality of a virus with the potential to take away the people I loved that brought death and loss to the forefront of my mind. I'm certain I'm not the only one who felt that way. I found that it made me appreciate the people in my circle a lot more, and the activities that I took for granted before we were told we couldn't do them anymore.

I'm grateful for the new awareness I have now around health and how to keep safe. It will certainly do me the world of good as I move through different stages of my health with my kidneys and surrounding health issues.

I think if the lockdowns came back, I'd be in a much better place to deal with it all. I use my logical brain a lot more now since it all began, I could reason with myself now about how to keep connected to people. I'm stronger now than I was and I'm happier in my own company. The only issue is that people with disabilities suffered in a way others didn't during Covid-19. We depend on daily services for things, similar to the way the elderly do to go to day centres and on outings. A lot was taken away from us very quickly. I think that the rush to protect everyone came on so fast that there simply wasn't time to sort out everything for people with additional needs. We had to sacrifice more than others I believe, but thankfully most things are back on track now. Also, the worry was there for the caregivers coming into your house, I didn't want to give anything to them, so it all became very hard. It was both amazing how much people cared about everyone's health during lockdowns, and very stressful because we were all so worried about making each other sick.

The uncertainty about what services might be removed for me if lockdowns come back is always a worry. There are a lot of services I depend on and to lose them again would be a big challenge. I'd find it very hard to go back to the way things were socially with not being able to meet people. Although I am a lot happier within myself, I'm still a very sociable person and I do need that to thrive.

All in all though, I think the government did the best they could. I would have liked to see masks come in a bit earlier, but I believe we did the best we could. They were trying to protect the nation and to do that, they had to treat everybody equally and they often had to make decisions at the last minute. There was a lot for them to be taking into consideration.

The only thing I think could have really been improved was access to doctors. People had to be really seriously ill to get to see a doctor and for someone with additional needs, it was nearly impossible. I did find that aspect of it all very frustrating. What I'm trying to say is that other illnesses didn't just disappear because we had Covid-19 lockdowns. People still needed to see doctors face to face for other things and that just didn't happen. I still don't think it's back to where it should be with seeing a doctor, but it definitely has improved.

Even though we were all in a little cocoon during Covid-19, I do feel that we were able to expand into the community cocoons in a way we couldn't have if we hadn't been in lockdown. I got involved in a networking group for business women during Covid-19 that I don't think I ever would have otherwise. Imagine, me, a business woman!! It was full of women who were interested in therapy and holistic things to get together via Zoom and support each other through difficult times. Each woman would come on and discuss their area of expertise and it really got me through. It gave me a structure and a purpose that would have been absent at that time. I learned a lot at that time from those meetings, I have a lot more knowledge now and have kept up a lot of those connections. I spent a huge amount of time doing different courses and widened my horizons, such as hypnotherapy and NLP. I wanted to use my time wisely, not sit around a go stir-crazy. It was a hard time in my life for sure, but I made it a fruitful time too.

I noticed a big increase in how much I was online during Covid-19, it was a Godsend to me to be able to video-call people during it all. It was the only thing that kept me connected to people during lockdowns. I know social media has its pitfalls, but for those purposes, it worked wonders for me. I became friends with people from all over the country. I tried to talk to as many people as possible just to keep myself busy and feel connected to the world somehow. I did feel there was a lack of support for people emotionally through Covid-19. The government were trying to protect our physical health but we couldn't just ring the doctor and say we were lonely as they had much more important stuff to be dealing with.

The thing is that if your mental and emotional health aren't great, your physical health is eventually going to suffer because of that. For that reason, I think we needed to focus more on the emotional impact of lockdowns at the time.

Not everybody would have had access to the internet, what about those people? What were they supposed to do to find some support? I think we need to go back to taking just 5 minutes to check in with each other, especially people who are vulnerable. I've had to let go of the expectation that just because I check in on people, that they will do the same for me. If I expected that all the time I would end up living in resentment. People do what they can and we are all busy.

I do think Covid-19 was meant to happen and it has taught me a lot. It took some things away from me and gave me some unexpected things that I'm grateful for. It has made me stronger as a person. Actually more than that, it has made me know myself more as a person and I like me! The aspects of my life that it took away at the time, I learned to navigate around and find alternatives and replacements for, like video calling instead of meeting. So, I've learned that I can adapt and cope in unprecedented times. I'm proud of myself for that. We have all come through this together and hopefully now we will never need to go back to that loneliness and isolation again.

CHAPTER 10

WHEN ALL IS SAID AND DONE

So, why did I write this book and what is my message now that you have reached the conclusion? Well, I guess there are several reasons I wrote it but the main reason is I want to leave a legacy. I want to build on the first book I wrote called 'Me and my Backbone'. No one wants to be a one hit wonder do they?

Let's talk about legacy and writing a book about life as a woman with disabilities who is determined to thrive and challenge stereotypes and orthodoxies. And trust me, I've tried to make this book humorous but insightful.

First things first, what is legacy? Is it a fancy word for leaving something behind after you're gone? Is it a fancy way of saying "I was here, people!"? Well, in a way, yes. But it's more than that. It's about the impact you leave behind. It's about *how* people remember you. It's about the stories they tell about you long after you're gone. And let's face it, we all want to be remembered for something good.

Now, let's talk about writing a book about life as a woman with disabilities. That's a tall order, my friends. But it's a necessary one. Why? Because we need more stories like mine. We need more voices like mine in the public space. We also need to challenge the stereotypes and orthodoxies that society has built around people with disabilities. And what better way to do that than to tell my story and, of course, your story?

Now, I know what you're thinking. "But I'm not a writer. I can barely string a sentence together." Well, my friends, let me tell you a secret. Nobody starts out as a great writer. It takes practice. A lot of practice. It takes patience. It takes a willingness to learn. And most importantly, it takes a willingness to make mistakes. Because let's face it, nobody's perfect. Not even Shakespeare.

But why bother writing a book in the first place? Why not just tell your story to your friends and family? Well, for starters, neither me, nor you, nor our friends and family will be around forever. And even if they were, they can only tell a story from a particular perspective. They can't tell it from mine or yours. And let's face it, our own perspectives are the ones that matter.

Plus, writing a book can be therapeutic. It can help you process your thoughts and feelings in a way that talking to someone can't. It can also help you gain a new perspective on your life. And who knows? Maybe your story can help someone else who's going through something similar as I hope my story will do.

But let's get back to the humour, shall we? Writing a book about life as a woman with my wide range of disabilities and, well, adventure-filled life was a real challenge. Especially as I've tried throughout to challenge stereotypes and orthodoxies at the same time. But that doesn't mean it can't be fun and you all know my motto by now...'Keep smiling aways.'

For example, have you ever noticed how people react when they see someone like me with a disability? It's like they've seen a unicorn or something! They either stare at you like you're some kind of tourist attraction, or they ignore you completely.

It's like they're afraid to acknowledge your existence. But here's the thing. You can use those moments to your advantage. You can use them as fuel for your writing. You can turn those awkward encounters into funny anecdotes. You can use them to challenge people's perceptions of what it means to have a disability. And who knows? Maybe you'll even make them laugh in the process.

Writing a book can also be a great way to educate people about the challenges that people with disabilities face.

Every day we are above ground is a learning day. Every day we have on this previous planet brings new potential. Life, my friends, is for living.

About the Author

Siobhán Mungovan

'True Beauty Consists Not In Beautiful Appearance But In Inner Beauty Of Character.' My name is Siobhán Mungovan. I am from Co Clare, Ireland. I am a Mind Coach, NLP Practitioner and Hypnotherapist.

Real beauty is an integral trait of one's nature and temperament. True beauty does not mean only physical appearance; it is also the beauty that lies inside a human being. I help and support women to turn inward and see the true beauty that lies within.

www.keepsmilingalways.ie

Acknowledgements

I would like to take this opportunity to thank the following people; my family and friends. I am the person I am today because of you all. You all encouraged me to reach for the stars in everything I have achieved in my life.

To my incredible talented writing team of Niall MacGiolla Bhuí from ShadowScript Ghostwriters and Anna Gray from Book Hub Publishing who have supported me every step of the way. You both have done such a terrific job of expressing my voice, my words and making them so eloquent. I have learnt so much from you both throughout this whole process.

To Book Hub Publishing and my senior editor, Susan McKenna, thanks for all the support you have shown me thoughout this whole project. There were days where I questioned myself and doubted my strength but you were always there by my side reminding me of my "Why". Thanks also to Book Hub reviewer, Amy Harrington, for her insightful comments.

To my Sponsors, Ei Electronics, Clare County Council and Spina Bifida Hydrocephalus Ireland - thank you all so much for supporting me and my book.

To Roger Leyden from RML Marketing & Business Development thank you for all your knowledge and expertise. It has been a pleasure working with you.

To the Renal Team at UHL. I am extremely grateful for all the medical support I have received throughout my life so far. I would like to give a special mention to my Nephrologist Dr Liam Casserly. I can't believe it's been 16 years since I first walked into your Consultancy room. As the years went on there is no doubt I have become that little bit more feisty! As a doctor, Dr Liam Casserly really does listen to his patients. Being heard by your doctor while living with chronic illness can make all the difference on the very tough days, so for that I am eternally grateful and can never express my appreciation enough.

Finally, I would like to thank you, the reader, since the publication of my first book "Me and My Backbone" in 2014. I've had the opportunity to meet the most incredible and inspiring human beings. You have given me the courage to speak on stages which, as a child, I could only have dreamt of. As you are about to go on this new journey with me I hope you get as much out of this book as I did writing it.